THE WISDOM
OF
SERPENTS

Reflections on
Religion and Foreign Policy

THE WISDOM OF SERPENTS

Reflections on Religion and Foreign Policy

by Roland Homet

Drawn from a multi-year, multidisciplinary,
inter-religious forum supported in part by the
Ruth Gregory Soper Memorial Fund

FORWARD MOVEMENT PUBLICATIONS
CINCINNATI, OHIO

2002

Copyright © 2001 by Roland Homet

Published by Forward Movement Publications
412 Sycamore Street
Cincinnati, Ohio 45202 USA

www.forwardmovement.org
1-800-543-1813

The serpent said to the woman, ". . . God knows that when you eat of [the fruit] your eyes will be opened, and you will be like God, knowing all things."

—Genesis 3:1-5

Jesus sent out his apostles to spread the good news, commanding them to be "wise as serpents and innocent as doves."

—Matthew 10:16

Table of Contents

Foreword

The report that follows was written in the spring of 2001, months before the detonation of religious terrorism upon the buildings and people of the United States. It may have something to say, all the same, about what could have driven the suicide attacks of September 11, not by way of an excuse for those actions but by way of a longer-range understanding.

Naval officers used to be expected to learn the difference between an excuse for their conduct—which was not admissible—and an explanation for it, which could prove instructive.

In this case what is needed is a grasp of the motivation, not just for the acts of the extremists, but for the support these aroused in the more moderate communities of faith whose belief systems would never countenance the mass taking of innocent human lives. If we cannot bring ourselves to understand that estrangement, we may never succeed in finding a productive remedy.

At issue here are the three major Western faiths, which grew up together and which share many cardinal points of belief. They also share a susceptibility to extremes, and a penchant for claims to superiority. In the Islamic world at present, material deprivation tends to be taken as a sign of spiritual merit, while in the Judeo-Christian world the incidents of prosperity tend to be taken as proof of God's preference. The resulting antagonisms are neither necessary nor useful.

Beyond visiting justice on the terrorists themselves, accordingly, room must be found for religious thoughtfulness on all sides, with accompanying moderation of the attitudes that get foreign policies tangled. The essay that follows offers an entry into that assessment.

—R.H.
October 2001

Preface

> Today self-pride and self-congratulation play too domi-
> nant a role in our nation's treatment of international
> affairs. We cannot expect to displace, but we can aim to
> counter, this disabling tendency. Beginning with sober
> dialogue among ourselves, and reaching out through the
> instruments of public discourse, we can seek to intro-
> duce a measure of mindfulness into policy choices that
> are now too often mindless.

That was the statement of purpose adopted in 1998 by the founders of the Forum on Religion and Foreign Policy, a deliberately diversified discussion group that goes out of existence with the publication of this report.

Its origins trace back to the production, in 1997, of a critical review of international economic sanctions as employed by the government of the United States. These were of concern to the Commission on Peace of the Episcopal Diocese of Washington, for their impact on the weak and the innocent; and also to a business group called USA Engage, for their randomly disruptive effect on trade and commerce. There was a meeting of the two houses, and the two minds, leading in September 1997 to the issuance of an "Exploratory Essay" on economic sanctions.

Those who experienced this process discovered it had value beyond the issue of sanctions. They thought it could help reform an outlook among policy makers of almost casual arrogance, which was deeply troublesome on both practical and theological levels. Americans like to think of ours as a godly nation. What had happened? Where had we gone wrong? And how could we get back to basics? Perhaps a joinder of perspectives, drawing on and extending the diversity of the first study group, could serve to answer those questions.

In the fall and winter of 1997-98, accordingly, the process and the make-up of the Forum on Religion and Foreign Policy were stitched together by a mixed but harmonious steering committee. These included (alphabetically):

- The Rev. Katharine Babson, Episcopal priest and international educator
- Donald Deline, international businessman and Baptist deacon
- Gail Harrison, Episcopalian and publicist for USA Engage
- Roland Homet, international lawyer, diplomat, and author
- Dr. Douglas Johnston, authority on religion and diplomacy
- Rodney MacAlister, international businessman and churchman
- Gerard Powers, international analyst, U.S. Catholic Conference
- The Rev. Robert Smylie, UN office of the Presbyterian Church

From the beginning there was a consensus around key points of objective, which became expressed in a project description:

> America is at loose ends about its proper place in the world. We have economic and political and military power, we may even be indispensable to getting things done, but we are not very clear about what those things should be.
>
> . . . The pertinence of our leading faith traditions has not diminished, but the currency we give them has. And yet a case can be made for the practicality of principle, for its capacity to keep us out of mischief and into usefulness.
>
> This view is not to be confused with the kind of theological assertiveness that finds simple answers and seeks to impose them on the policy process. Typically that approach ignores critical nuances of thought and conduct, and admits no questions about the blunt policies it favors; it has become part of the problem and not of the solution.
>
> The Forum looks for ways of recovering spiritual direction. We favor the traditional religious values of modesty, realism, balance, and harmony. And we aim to combine these with foreign-policy effectiveness, in the long-term national interest.

To these ends, the steering committee decided on a set of procedures that persisted throughout the life of the Forum. It established, to begin with, an invited discussion group made up of accomplished international lawyers and business people, diplomats, scholars, non-profit leaders, and clergy. Membership spanned the breadth of the Abrahamic faiths, including Christians

(Catholics and Protestants), Muslims and Jews. This was an inquiry group: No one with an axe to grind was invited to take part. (*For a full list of participants, see Annex A.*)

Discussion was stimulated by a series of highly qualified presenters, covering a range of topics. These were offered as occasion and availability permitted; there was no *a priori* judgment as to what would prove important or in what sequence. Each session began with a presentation of 20 minutes duration, after which there was table-wide discussion in which the presenter did **not** take part; he or she was thereafter given ten closing minutes to sum up decisive points. (*For a full list of presenters and their topics, see Annex B.*)

Summaries of discussion were prepared in each case, for review and revision by the presenter. These were distributed to participants, including an array of interested persons around the country and abroad who received copies of all Forum materials. The Internet was employed to post the summaries, and other readings, on the Forum's website. (*For a full list of these documents and how to retrieve them, see Annex C.*)

To qualify for foundation support, the Forum's organizers incorporated in the District of Columbia and applied for, and received, nonprofit certification from the IRS. The fees for these steps, plus the costs of operation in the first year, were underwritten by voluntary member contributions. Expenses were spared through the provision of meeting space by a corporate member and, for a time, by the nonprofit U.S.-Russia Trade and Business Council. In the ensuing two years, financial support was generously granted by the Ruth Gregory Soper Memorial Fund, administered by the Episcopal Diocese of Washington. For its purposes, the Forum was seen as pursuing a new ministry which could be of value to the church at large.

This brought the group into contact with diocesan parishes, eight of which supported the grant application and four of which invited presentations from the Forum's director. Given the wealth of experience and interest in world affairs in the Washington area, these appearances were well-attended and provoked valuable discussion, which was then fed back into regular Forum proceedings.

The director also attended, and brought back to the group, conferences organized by the Inter-American Development Bank and by the Divinity School of the University of Chicago. Both of these sessions—"Culture Matters" and "The Sacred and the Sovereign"—contributed valuably to Part Two of this report.

The Forum stretched its wings further by creating a press breakfast series, with U.S. reporters who cover international affairs for print and broadcast media. Each month, presenters to the Forum would be asked also to talk informally with these correspondents at a 7:30 breakfast. The idea was for the press people to enlarge their circles of qualified experts while also broadening their sense of foreign policy choices. The discourse was useful for the Forum and also sometimes for the journalists, as in articles on our topics by Jane Perlez of the *New York Times* and Steven Mufson of the *Washington Post*. (*For a full list of press participants, see Annex D.*)

Along the way the Forum developed helpful ties to other, well-established institutions that furnished ideas and participants as well as website linkages. These included the Institute of World Affairs in Washington, the Watson Institute at Brown University, and the Woodstock Theological Center at Georgetown University. In addition, the Public Religion Project at the University of Chicago provided a steady stream of pertinent e-mail commentary, and the Virginia Theological Seminary opened its doors to an illuminating Forum debate on debt relief for the poorer nations.

The Forum's founders decided from the outset that it should have a three-year life. On January 29, 2001, accordingly, the last group discussion took place, focused on what should happen next. The group chose to create a repository of its papers, accessible to anyone with entry to the Internet, and to make clear that anyone was at liberty to pick up and follow its format. The present report, which is intended for wide distribution, may serve among other things as such an invitation.

The report has many contributors, as has been shown, but only one author. Anyone's insights are inevitably shaped by his or her own lifetime of thought and experience, which are not quite the same as for anyone else. I have been much enriched and disciplined by the shared experience of the Forum, but what I make of it is my responsibility.

Roland Homet
Forum director
April, 2001

PART ONE

Religion

CHAPTER 1

The Range of Christian Attitudes

For over ten years, since the end of the Cold War, America's foreign policy has been guided by little more than a wave of self-congratulation. The God of our forefathers would not care for that. It is not good for us as a people, and it is not useful for us as a country.

Religious principle can be overplayed in public life. But it has its place; for good or ill it serves to shape our attitudes, and from attitudes come public policies. The aim in this study is to examine foreign policy through the lens of American public attitudes.

There is not just one religious tradition in America but several, both within and beyond Christianity. Across all these traditions there appear to be three main attitudinal choices: Triumphal, Beneficent, and Modest. Each has its own signature and its own sway.

Triumphal

Coming off of the Cold War, and capped by the overwhelming U.S. and allied triumph in the Persian Gulf

War, there is a tendency to see the world today in polar terms with the Good forces (us) having prevailed over the Bad (others). On top of that, the American Creed with its political and economic attractions—often stated in shorthand terms as Market Democracy—seems to many people both here and abroad to have attained a near-religious standing and to command a faith-like devotion. This can be understood, but it is both ill-advised and hazardous.

A religion built on human achievement tends to displace the Higher Power that the Bible tells us repeatedly we need to be able to turn to for the correction of human flaws. A polarized view of the world, moreover, veers in the direction of the early Christian Manichean heresy, with its long-discredited moral absolutism. And a belief that we are vested with superior capacity to control events and people comes close to the amorality of *realpolitik*, which the ancient Greek historian Thucydides once described as something that allows the strong to do what they can while the weak accept what they must. That is not in the greater American tradition.

Beneficent

Compassion for others is in that tradition, and is broadly favored. Political liberals and conservatives alike seek to extend American ideals to those we think would profit from them. This is not just an exercise of power, but has a long missionary tradition behind it. Nonetheless it can be and has been overdone.

The Gnostic heresy of the early church held that one nation or one people can be specially favored instruments of God's will to teach and perfect others. This, plainly, is arrogance; and it does not sit well with those toward whom it is directed. Mohandas Gandhi developed the point, arguing that what the human race needs is not more proselytizing but rather that, "Hindus become better Hindus and Mussulmans become better Mussulmans and Christians become better Christians." This would yield, he thought, better relations and surer religion. It is up to God, not man, to judge the quality of human devotion.

Modest

A third alternative, now growing in favor, moves beyond domination and beyond paternalism to Christian humility—not the breast-beating type but the quiet sort that concerns itself with effectiveness more than with self-imagery. This bases its judgments, however imperfectly, on interests rather than ideology, recognizing as past heresies have taught us that *disinterested* intrusion is more likely than self-interest to propel us into usurping the role of God.

There are those who assert that this course is not open to America, that we are a "Wilsonian nation" and must be ready to react "when our principles and our values are offended." There is a difference, however, between offense to our feelings and injury to our interests. The deep tradition of Christian modesty, or Christian realism as it is sometimes called, directs its response to the latter. This leaves room in wider arenas for the will of God, and history, to make their mark.

CHAPTER 2

Roots and Repercussions

Triumphalism

Polarization, or "us" versus "them," finds warrant of a sort in apocalyptic literature. The book of Revelation, in particular, with its battle at Armageddon, portrays the final destruction of an evil foe. But we need to remember that, when this was written, Christianity was a tiny embattled sect appealing to God for vindication against the overwhelming forces of Rome. For the United States, as the world's surviving superpower—today's Rome—to adopt such a perspective would be a reversal of Revelation.

Paul's Epistle to the Romans points in another direction:

> Beloved, never avenge yourselves, but leave room for
> the wrath of God; for it is written, "Vengeance is mine,
> I will repay, says the Lord." (Romans 12:19)

Yet religious zeal, along with political ambition, have often overridden this admonition. It is useful to recall that Stalin was a seminarian, as are many of the Taliban in present-day Afghanistan. Christian nations and peoples have been caught up, historically, in the destructive frenzy of the Crusades and of the Inquisition. The Empires of Rome and Spain and England, among others, have wielded the "white man's burden" (Rudyard Kipling) against perceived and presumed lesser people. America today, willy-nilly, hefts its own empire, and attitudes of condescension tend to go with that position.

But there are also counterweights in literature and opinion. America was founded in reaction to oppression, whether religious or political, and there have always been voices to remind us of that heritage. One such powerful voice was Herman Melville, whose Captain Ahab proclaimed himself a power against God himself: "I am a prophet and a fulfiller. Who is over me?" Melville's answer was to see to it that Ahab was defeated in the end, not vindicated.

Beneficence

Mother Teresa famously advised us that we are to hold ourselves open to commissions from God. "God has only our hands," she said, "with which to bless the world." But we are not to be so certain of our appointments that we start regarding them as our right. That is the lesson of Eden and of Babel as well. As Biblical scholars put it, "the Kingdom of God . . . is something which God gives, not something which men 'build.' It is not a Utopia or a new social order."

Ignoring that lesson leads policy in the direction of what National Public Radio has called "Liberal Humanitarian Imperialism." It is the imperialism charge that stings. But doing good can in fact bring harm, just as a child's helping a butterfly out of its cocoon can kill or maim the insect. H.L. Mencken once wrote that "for every human problem there is a solution that is simple, neat, and wrong." This is the course to be avoided, by accepting that we may not know what we do.

Otherwise we can find ourselves believing that our good intentions alone have a positive, settling effect. The most searing recent example of that misconception was at Srebrenica, in Yugoslavia, when the United States used its chairmanship of the UN Security Council to push through a resolution declaring that city a "safe area," without any provision of a military nature to make it so. In consequence, the Serbs swept through the area and massacred its inhabitants. It is the presumptuousness that lingers: God's voice may ordain, but man's mere dictate cannot.

Modesty

The teaching of Ecclesiasticus is that:

Sovereignty passes from nation to nation
On account of injustice and insolence and wealth.
How can dust and ashes be proud?

Ecclesiasticus (Sirach) 10:8-9

God, not man, disposes. Even as awesome a power as King Belshazzar of Babylon had to read God's "handwriting on the wall" and discover his dismissal. The mighty ruler was weighed and found wanting, in the prophetic reading by Daniel.

Today there is no general call for a Pax Americana of comparable power or authority. Some things we favor in the world are likely to occur without our help, others will develop despite our opposition. "The challenge," as Robert L. Hutchings has written, "will be to engage in those areas and on those issues where important American interests are at stake and where a publicly sustainable level of commitment can make a difference."

Disregard of such advice creates a specter of hegemony—for modern America as for ancient Persia—which others, even friends, are moved to resist. Our secondary boycotts to drive allies into line with U.S. policy, our insistence on harsh and ineffectual economic sanctions around the globe, our unilateral pursuit of nuclear-missile defense: all of these and more create a backlash that can lead major nations to gang up in opposition. Weaker peoples may go further and mount terrorist responses. American interests, which need cooperative support, can only suffer. History suggests that this is a matter not just of human limitation but of God's design.

In religious belief systems, God ultimately rules and man does not. Hegemons stumble. We humans are given not just muscles, but a mind; not just viscera, but a heart. We are each of us more stewards than soldiers, more servants than rulers. That is settled theology, and it is also a sound basis for foreign policy. It is grounded in modesty, in realism, in humility.

Authorities

Humility is at the core of the Judeo-Christian tradition. The prophet Micah summed up centuries of observance when he wrote:

> ...what does the Lord require of you
> but to do justice, and to love kindness,
> and to walk humbly with your God? (Micah 6:8)

Jesus of Nazareth, in time, added his voice:

> ...all who exalt themselves will be humbled,
> but all who humble themselves will be exalted.
> (Luke18:14)

Jesus acted out this injunction in his own life, declining the temptation to revise the political order of his day and submitting himself instead to the cross.

His admonition to those who follow has been, "Do not judge so that you may not be judged" (Matt 7:1). One who took that guidance clearly to heart was Pope John XXIII, who held back his own ruling hand with the caution, "Observe everything, ignore much, correct little."

The practice of spiritual modesty is entrenched as well in American political traditions. George Washington's Farewell Address advised his countrymen to avoid being driven by emotions in their foreign relations, and to base them instead on enlightened self-interest. John Quincy Adams, when still Secretary of State, wrote that, "America is the well-wisher to the freedom and independence of all. She is the champion and vindicator only of her own." Abraham Lincoln, speaking at Independence Hall in 1861, said that American values can best impress themselves abroad by the power of example and not imposition.

In our own time General George Marshall, as portrayed by Walter Lippmann, said we must "give up the attempt to control events which we do not have the power or knowledge to control." And George F. Kennan, writing as recently as 1999, stated that "this whole tendency to see ourselves as the center of political enlightenment and as teachers to a great part of the world strikes me as unthought-through, vainglorious and undesirable."

There is a long diplomatic as well as religious history behind this view. Put simply, invitation works better than intrusion. Francois de Callieres, diplomatic historian to then-superpower King Louis XIV, summed up the matter when he wrote: "Success achieved by force or imposition rests on an insecure foundation; whereas success based on reciprocal advantage promises further successes."

The scholar who best embodies the convergence of these two traditions, religious and diplomatic, is the theologian Reinhold Niebuhr. In his most noted work, *The Children of Light and the Children of Darkness*, Niebuhr allowed that America has done good things in the world, "but we are still inclined to pretend that our power is exercised by a peculiarly virtuous nation. The uniqueness of our virtue," he commented, "is questioned by both our friends and our enemies." For him the children of light, the committed idealists among us, are more to be watched than the lackadaisical or the self-willed. For what is needed is not zeal but humility:

> The real point of contact between democracy and profound religion is in the spirit of humility which democracy requires and which must be one of the fruits of religion.

A similar idea is offered in Niebuhr's *Serenity Prayer*, so widely used today that most reciters probably do not know the name of its author. In short form, the prayer asks: "God, grant me the serenity to accept the things I cannot change, the courage to change the things I can, and the wisdom to know the difference." The longer form continues: "Taking, as Jesus did, this sinful world as it is and not as I would have it . . ." It takes true humility to leave error uncorrected.

Other thinkers have followed in this path, among them Kennan, himself a devoted churchman. Walter McDougall, author of the highly pertinent *Promised Land, Crusader State* (1997), wrote in *Orbis* the following year:

> [T]o expect utopian results from diplomacy and war is inevitably to invite immoral consequences. . . . A truly moral approach to statecraft, therefore, takes human nature as it is, respects limits, and acknowledges the contingency of all human creations.

An earlier book of theology called *U.S. Foreign Policy and Christian Ethics* (1977) asserted that "Our best leaders have never thought of imposing our ideals...on other nations. There has been, however, an American messianism that does not shrink from this.... We serve our ideals best when we are more humble; when we abandon the self-righteous pose that has been a blight on our role in the world." Even that injunction, the authors thought, was a moral principle calling in its application for humility and restraint.

Balance

As that admonition suggests, what is wanted here is not so much a final settlement of the argument as even-handedness in its application. Thus we may look to employ, in American foreign policy—

- both ideals and interests
- both engagement and detachment
- both power and restraint

Robert Osgood's classic 1953 study, *Ideals and Self-Interest in America's Foreign Relations*, is clear on the first point. It says that as a country we have acted responsibly, and well, whenever our "ideals and self-interest [have] coincided." Jean Anouilh's historical play *Becket* likewise cherishes a time when "the honor of God and the honor of country come together." By clear implication, if either of these attributes is missing, detachment is the proper course.

Detachment is what helps us stay out of embroilments that do not concern us. It is itself a spiritual quality, separating man's proper realm from God's. But engagement can also be a tool in pursuit of balance, as a means of understanding others and of protecting our true concerns. We may not, for example, be able to reorder Chinese society, but we can monitor the rules of fair trade and we can guard against undue shifts in the regional balance of power.

The possession of military and economic and political power, for a country in our global position, can be as important as restraint in its use. There are small countries and large that rely on the United States to prevent bullying by others, or as a warrant for keeping their own forces small. There is no present case, therefore, for discarding our sabers; but there is a case for not rattling them.

Some qualities can be named that do us no good and that, in pursuit of spiritual balance, we ought simply to give up. These include, prominently, judgmentalism and condescension. People everywhere are drawn to American example, even in difficult circumstances; but they reject and resent being talked down to. On grounds of utility as well as principle, we ought to try something else.

There are in fact three elements that could make up the core of a revised public attitude, responsive to America's global needs and to our religious heritage. These roughly parallel the three parts of the Serenity Prayer. We could learn to: (1) tolerate conduct that does not threaten us; (2) focus on real threats as priorities for response; and (3) strive to understand what motivates other people. Beyond that, we could learn to listen more and not be too sure we are right.

CHAPTER 3

Islamic and Judaic Counterparts

Christianity is part of the Abrahamic covenant, subscribed to by the three great monotheistic religions that trace their origins back to the God-invited migration of Abraham and his family into what was to become the Holy Land. There are differences among them, but also shared values and experiences that may help generate common approaches to some aspects of global relations.

Extremism

All three religions have undergone bursts of exclusivity, driven by fear and ignorance as well as self-righteousness. (The interpenetration of church and state has tended to make things worse.) Among Jews, the book of Ezra documents the post-Exile banishment of non-Jewish wives and children. This is counterbalanced in the Hebrew Testament by the book of Ruth, celebrating the Moabite ancestry of the great King David. But the persistence into our time of extremist sentiment toward others is manifested by such radically obsessive anti-Arab figures as Rabbi Meir David Kahane and his son, both assassinated for their pains.

Within Islam, there are both radical and moderate elements, sometimes drawing on the same Qur'anic sources. The concept of *jihad*, or holy war, is endorsed in the Qur'an as a defensive measure against those who seek to destroy the Muslim religion. It is also employed by the more extreme elements of the faith to justify preemptive strikes against alien societies. The operative myth here is the counter-Crusade, seeking to undo that ancient grievance.

Radical sentiment in both cases is aggravated by the objective realities of beleaguerment. Judaism is a dwindling religion in terms of global numbers, and its homeland is under constant assault. This can help explain why press and political comment on the Palestinian *intifada* is so remarkably one-sided, extolling Jewish snipers and reviling Arab rock throwers. It is a case, for the Jews, of feeling they have their backs to the sea.

Islam, by contrast, is a global religion with vast numbers of adherents. Among the world's historical powers, however, it stands out for never yet having repaired the decline in its former political ascendance. This is frustrating, particularly when coupled with perceived condescension from today's dominant powers, including the United States. A terrible sense of disappointment underlies Islamic retaliatory movements.

Mercy

But these are not the only or even the dominant strains in the two faiths. The overarching theme of the

Qur'an, as of the Bible, is mercy rather than meanness. There is for example the long-standing Abrahamic tradition of hospitality to strangers, which visitors to the Holy Land can readily experience. "Aggressive" mercy on the Western model is blessedly absent from these beleaguered peoples, who lack the capacity to impose their sympathy.

Modesty

Despite the fact that all three faith traditions, including Christianity, have done battle with each other and within themselves, each in its own way has been drawn to pay homage to the higher values of restraint and reconciliation. In fact, an effort to constrain coercive force has been seen by all three as necessary to counter the "holy war" excesses that have afflicted them all. The very inhumanity of religious zeal on such occasions is what has spawned the Just War principles, examined later, which have been adopted in some way by each.

Judaism is a world religion not because of its numbers but because of its principles of sustainable justice and morality, reaching back to the Ten Commandments. Torah, tradition, and observance have set standards for the world and—sometimes uncomfortably—for the Jewish community itself. These rules of behavior can be defter and less oppressive than the Christian versions that have followed. The "silver rule," for example, commended by the great Jewish commentator Rabbi Hillel, says: "What is hateful to you, do not do to anyone"— which compares favorably on the scale of restraint with the relatively intrusive Golden Rule.

The religion of Islam, despite deviation by some adherents, is noteworthy for its precepts favoring cultural and religious pluralism. There is today, in addition, an insufficiently noticed resurgence of the moderate and tolerant Muslim practices that follow those precepts. As the newer generation of leaders approaches power in places like Egypt, they have been heard to promise a restrained application of Islamic law, or *sharia*. This is a sign of the important difference between fundamentalism, which can be marked by revenge, and revivalism which charts a constructive course.

Chapter 4

Applying Religious Guidance

Secular society gives signs these days of wanting to find principled guidelines for conduct. This is evident in such advanced fields as biomedicine and information transfer, where technical expertise alone can seem inadequate to the challenges presented. In foreign policy, however, the tendency since World War II has been to dwell on the intricacies of power relationships, which tends to confer authority on a mandarin class. It can be difficult in this setting to find room for religious guidance, yet religion is uniquely capable of engaging power in a way that is understandable to all.

In the mid-1980s, the Roman Catholic, Episcopal and Methodist churches each conducted influential studies of nuclear arms control that put human attitudes ahead of technology as the determinant of sound policy. Their reports derived sensible rules of behavior from human nature, its limitations, and its connection to God. That approach made a contribution then, and it can do so again.

Rules and Reflections

Over the centuries, in Jewish and Islamic as well as Christian traditions, the case for restraint in the use of external coercion has been solidified into firm—though not always fully respected—prescriptions. These are the so-called Just War principles, three of which may be cited to illustrate the whole. An exercise of force may be justified, these principles say, only if it is:

- capable of achieving more good than harm (proportional)
- reasonably likely to attain its positive ends (effective), and
- fought with just means, sparing noncombatants (focused).

Unless the coercion is proportional, effective, and focused, it will not pass Just War muster.

There are places where religious guidance of this sort is regularly applied to international behavior. The Davos World Economic Forum, for example, each year hosts sessions on religion and society. The Italian lay Catholic community of Sant' Egidio is known for its conferences on that subject. And the meetings in Catalonia on relations between Islam and the West routinely include theologians from both sides.

What is needed now is to probe further, and to address the issue not just of force but of Imperial Overstretch as it is described in this account. That will entail the curbing of arrogance, which is a matter of attitude, which is in turn the province of religion.

Jesus spoke to this constellation of issues when he

told his followers to "be wise as serpents and innocent as doves." But what in fact is the wisdom of serpents, and how should it partake of the innocence of doves?

One thing we can be clear about is that we need for our wisdom to open itself to the judgment of God. That was the encouragement of Eden, which Jesus seems by his formulation to have accepted. But only if it is God's judgment that we adopt, and not an arrogation by mankind. Innocence in this sense can serve to check wisdom, by keeping it humble. Yet wisdom also can work to check innocence, by examining the consequences of a given action and not just its possible good intentions.

So, deeds undertaken to make ourselves feel momentarily good would not qualify. This caution by itself should tend to rule out a fairly wide swath of current American conduct, as we shall see. Ineffectual, offensive actions would have to be abandoned. But first we would have to be honest about our digressions. We would have to "clean up our act."

Of Law and Language

There is a tendency in U.S. foreign policy to maintain that our actions are justified by international law, or by the UN Charter, or by U.S. law, or by special facts and circumstances, when none of these things may be true. In the invasion of Grenada, to pick that example, the U.S. claimed that the attack was needed to free U.S. hostages when we knew in advance that they were being released. In other cases, we have issued or endorsed feel-good pronouncements that we knew were untenable—Srebrenica's "safe area" edict being only one of these. In 1993 alone, the *New York Times* counted 181 such declarations. Neither serpent nor dove would approve such behavior.

"Hypocrisy," we are told, "is the homage that vice pays to virtue." In so doing, of course, it aligns itself with vice. There is no room for religious direction in this framework.

The heedless dispersal of law and language is ultimately a threat to all—including, notably, smaller states that rely on the shelter of reality and truth. Bullies may ignore such safeguards but God-fearing people cannot.

There is a religious play, Robert Bolt's "A Man for All Seasons," that makes this point. It puts the endangered Sir Thomas More in a conversation with his son-in-law, Roper, who wants More to bend the law to his own protective use. More resists, giving rise to this colloquy:

> Roper: So now you'd give the Devil benefit of the law!
>
> More: Yes. What would you do? Cut a great road through the law to get after the Devil?
>
> Roper: I'd cut down every law in England to do that!
>
> More: Oh? (Advances on Roper.) And when the last law was down, and the Devil turned round on you—where would you hide, Roper, the laws all being flat? . . . Do you really think you could stand upright in the winds that would blow then?

There is a passage in Shakespeare's "Troilus and Cressida" that speaks to the hazards of disregarding vital distinctions when pronouncing policy:

Take but degree away, untune that string
And hark what discord follows!
. . . Then everything includes itself in power,
Power into will, will into appetite:
And appetite, an universal wolf,
So doubly seconded with will and power,
Must make perforce an universal prey,
And last eat up himself.

We shall need to be attentive to such risks.

— PART TWO —

Foreign Policy

Chapter 5

Role of the Church

Historically and Today

Western diplomacy as currently practiced was developed in good part within the Church. The Pope and his bishops were not just witnesses to global relations but a shaping factor in them. Historians of the era, which ran from the 4th to the 16th centuries, speak of the "ultramontane" (beyond the nearby hills) policies of the Church, which was at the time inseparable from the State. The leaders of both were concerned to make real results happen, through insistence when necessary but through foresight and persuasion when possible.

The tendency of the modern and disentangled church, however, has been to content itself with proclamation. At national and international as well as at diocesan level, religious spokesmen on public policy matters often act as if it were enough to adopt a resolution and go home. In August 2000, at a Millennium World Peace Summit of Religious and Spiritual Leaders convened at the United Nations, the leaders signed a broadly worded document that offered no way of realizing its hopes. Dr. Lawrence E. Sullivan, director of the Harvard Center for the Study of World Religions, remarked that if the religious wanted to make an impact, they would have to "go to school on the issues" in a way that did not happen there and does not usually happen. If one wishes to enact innocence, he might have said, one must couple it with wisdom.

Extra-Religious Influence

The Church can make a difference, when it chooses, in foreign policy matters that touch upon religious values. It did so in 2000 by lobbying successfully for debt relief for the poorest nations. Church leaders and servants worked in the trenches to acquaint policy makers with the choices and to press for humane outcomes. Both the Democratic and Republican nominees for President ultimately came down in favor of those positions, and the needed rules were adopted both by the U.S. and by other creditors. These included anti-corruption and pro-development features aimed at avoiding repetition.

The serpent and the dove can work together.

Inter-Religious Settlements

Religious wars have been a feature of the political landscape throughout history, and remain so today. Can they be defused through the application of shared religious traditions, or is this expecting too much? There are things to be said on both sides of that question. Jerusalem is a holy site for all three Abrahamic religions, which has made it a flash point for rivalries between them. It might also make that city a proving ground for shared values such as justice and mercy. To date, however, it is largely the secular dialogues in the region that have managed to build confidence and understanding. Religious peace initiatives seem not to be able to move away from anger and hostility.

The other side of the coin is that secular efforts, by themselves, have not moved matters very far toward peace. Religious considerations—which are traditionally ignored or devalued in most mediation efforts—are insufficient for reconciliation but may be necessary to it.

NGO Intercession

Spiritual and temporal mediation can take place outside the church, but using similar values, through the medium of non-governmental organizations (NGO). Douglas Johnston, editor of *Religion, The Missing Dimension of Statecraft*, has founded the International Center for Religion and Diplomacy to capitalize on this opportunity. The Center's mission statement proposes "serving as a bridge between politics and religion in support of peacemaking," by "deploying multi-skilled, inter-religious teams to address actual or incipient conflicts." The serpent and dove can forage together.

Non-governmental interventions in dispute resolution may sometimes work where official intrusions do not. "Doctors Without Borders," of French origin, has had a stunning success whereas diplomacy without borders (as we shall see) has failed. NGO engagement in such pursuits is typically a long-term process, building confidence beyond the attainment of particular objectives.

The groups involved must avoid letting their enthusiasm outrun their competence; indeed, they must build their competence in a continuing way. But with that understanding, they can serve as spurs to the building of civil society, and hence of internal mediation capacity, around the world.

CHAPTER 6

Diplomatic Detachment

We move now to official diplomacy—which will always have its place, and probably pride of place—to consider what features are necessary to make it both more successful and more true to America's purpose.

America's Role

We are not the world's anointed justice giver. Laying down rules of conduct is acceptable when the U.S. either responds to an invitation or acts in defense of its own vital interests; but more and more, that is not the case and our posture arouses both resistance and resentment. There is value in such cases in adopting an attitude of detachment. This is what separates interests from emotions, man's realm from God's.

Theologically speaking, the question is whether and when reform of other nations and peoples is an American prerogative. Those who, like us, have been favored by history, certainly should "give back." But what, specifically, is called for? Not, presumably, to usurp God's place as a justice giver; not to make conditions worse, or to become part of the problem; not to be arrogant or ineffective.

Instead of forcing God's hand, or history's, we would be better advised to submit to their patient seasons. For "accepting the things we cannot change" turns out to be good diplomacy as well as good religion. It serves the long-run interests of this country.

Exceptionalism

There is, it must be said, a strong current of opposing views. In the South Carolina primary of February 2000, insurgent candidate John McCain gave voice to those views when he said that America is a "Wilsonian" nation and added: "We can never say that a nation driven by Judeo-Christian principles will only intervene where our interests are threatened, because we also have values. And those values are very important." Indeed they are; the only question is whether they are exportable by force.

The origins of that question can be traced back a good deal farther than Woodrow Wilson, whose idealism gave it high visibility. America's founders liked to point to the Christian Testament as the root of this nation's exceptionalism. We were not like the scheming princes we had left behind. Instead we were "the light of the world... a city built on a hill [which] cannot be hid." (Matthew 5:14) We would do what was right and not what was expedient.

But, as an integral part of that perspective, we would not impose those high moral views on anyone else. Leave us alone, we said, and we would not trouble you. Our motto in those early days, when we thought we knew and were following God's will, was "Don't Tread on Us." Today, unfortunately, when we have to a degree lost that certainty, it is closer to "We'll Tread on You." That is not in keeping with America's history or its founding purpose.

We could withdraw from the world in the 18th century, and send a beacon light of our good example across the waters to any who freely chose to follow it. Now we are inescapably drawn into the world, by modern technology and economics, and the challenge is one of being true to ourselves as well as useful.

— CHAPTER 7 —

Balance of Powers

Keeping a balance among the military powers of the world is an ancient peace-keeping device that has survived into modern times. Partly it is necessary, in a dangerous environment, but partly too it is doing God's work. The historian Walter McDougall put the point well:

> . . . [T]he sort of reasonable, restrained, balance-of-power system founded in Westphalia, promoted by philosophers such as Hugo Grotius, Samuel Puffendorf, and Immanuel Kant, and nurtured by such hard-headed diplomats as Talleyrand, Metternich, and Palmerston, was not the *antithesis* of a Christian politics, but rather was the *best possible expression* of it, especially by contrast to the "religious" wars that preceded it and the even more wicked era of nationalist and ideological wars that followed. (Emphasis in original.)

Fr. Bryan Hehir, who now heads the Harvard Divinity School, believes that there is a largely unarticulated choice between two views of a Great Power's responsibility. Either it can confine itself to keeping a global balance among the major powers, or it can add to that such other tasks as humanitarian intervention. The question is whether in practice one can add such burdens and

34

still satisfy our proper mission. We will be looking into that issue. But first we need to examine current challenges to the balance of power itself.

NATO Expansion

A first wave of East European countries, including Poland and Hungary, was admitted to membership in an expanded NATO in 1998. There are now nine candidates for further admission, including seven that border immediately on Russia. Under Article 5 of the North Atlantic Treaty, these present and prospective members will be entitled to the full protective shield of NATO armament. But at least three of them, the Baltic states, are so situated that they can only be defended by nuclear strikes. The implications of this arrangement, like the U.S. policy of NATO expansion generally, have yet to be addressed in general debate.

NATO itself is being altered by these dispositions. It is moving from a highly focused regional defense alliance to one with a looser, more roving commission. It has taken on peacekeeping assignments outside its borders. Its deterrent and planning functions are beginning to migrate, against U.S. resistance, to the Western European Union in which we will no longer have a leadership position. All this is a direct consequence of American policies.

The balance-of-power effects could be substantial. NATO was created, in Lord Ismay's memorable phrase, to "keep the Russians out, the Germans down, and the Americans in." It is at least not clear that we have passed that era. To keep the peace now, it would make more sense to let the European Union serve as the vehicle for regional integration. This would be a matter of years rather than months, but its very slowness would allow collective military as well as economic competence to develop within Europe at a non-destabilizing pace.

The precipitate nature of American decision-making on this issue has generated opposition from some 90 percent of the U.S. foreign-policy elite. But their voice has been as nothing compared to the anticipated Polish vote in major U.S. cities. This is politically understandable, but is not consistent with sound policy.

Missile Defense

The United States has committed itself to a task of developing, and if possible deploying, a missile system that in the first instance can detect and destroy incoming missiles from a small belligerent force. There may be reason for such a course, in that smaller belligerents are less likely than larger ones to be deterred by nuclear counterforce; that was a lesson from the 1962 Cuban Missile Crisis, when Cuba declared itself willing to risk all in a preemptive strike and was restrained by its Soviet patrons. But the proposal nonetheless disturbs the balance of power in a number of important ways.

The Europeans and the Russians, to begin with, see missile defense as an attack on the linchpin of arms restraint, the ABM Treaty of 1972, which bolsters deterrence among the major powers by its preservation of retaliatory capacity against any first strike; a missile shield, to the extent it is effective or is believed by its possessor to be so, would undo that assurance. If the U.S. abandons the treaty, as we currently threaten to do, the Russians would be free to renounce the START II nuclear arms reductions they had previously agreed to. Both Russians and Europeans see this as deeply destabilizing.

The U.S. plan has also, and especially, estranged the Chinese because even the limited U.S. system now being proposed would neutralize their small nuclear force and free the United States (in their eyes) to champion Taiwan. If the Chinese react by expanding their nuclear arms, it will distort the regional balance among other Asian nations like Pakistan, India, and Japan.

There is a hope among some American experts that pushing missile defense may induce China or Russia, or both, to offer a build-down of missile strengths as a price for eliminating the U.S. system. This seems like a high-risk game to be playing with nuclear weapons. One must ask whether the hoped-for results are worth such risks. Particularly is this so as the U.S. system is being offered in the domestic political arena as a rescuer from all our insecurities. It may be hard to withdraw that pabulum.

The desire to gain nuclear impregnability stems from a nostalgia for the days when our country was an untouched fortress on a hill. But the sense of security being sought is a false one, since as a technical and financial matter no system is operable or in sight of becoming so. And even if one could be built and made to work, it would not meet the challenge of suitcases or other small delivery vehicles. These alternatives are less costly and more reliable; they are what a small belligerent might be expected to employ.

Hegemony and Its Frailties

Missile defense is an instance of the go-it-alone propensity that currently threatens to dominate foreign policy in the United States. We seek to steamroll others into following our lead, in default of which we threaten to proceed by ourselves. Little thought seems given to side effects or to adverse consequences of this approach. What our country most needs, for itself and for others, is a freely shared consensus and not just an acquiescence.

Josef Joffe, the highly regarded editor of the German weekly *Die Zeit,* addressed himself to this point in a column:

> Ten years after victory in the Cold War, the United States is still No. 1 by any conceivable measure. But the lesser actors—Russia, Europe, China—are beginning to make true what history and political theory have predicted all along: Great power will generate "ganging up." Nos. 2, 3 and 4 will seek to balance against Mr. Big.
>
> [Recently], President Vladimir Putin of Russia swept into Berlin, where he deftly executed a classic gambit of Muscovite diplomacy. This is the age-old attempt to forge privileged relations with Germany, the traditional holder of the European balance. He wooed, and he won.
>
> . . . Subtly and cautiously, the lesser players are acting out the oldest game of nations. Primacy provokes, and power begets power. What is No. 1 to do?
>
> One assumes that "the last remaining superpower" will want to remain one. But if so, the United States might recall the best tradition of its postwar grand strategy. It wasn't just sheer size and weight that shaped this most brilliant chapter of American diplomacy. It was the bipartisan conviction that power comes with responsibility,

and that responsibility must defy short-term self-interest or the domestic fixation of the day.

. . . Great powers remain great if they promote their own interests by serving those of others.

Egocentrism can generate difficulties, whether it shows up in heedless militarism or in thoughtless ideology. Scholars tell us that triumphalism in either form is a profound source of conflict between the West and the rest. Whoever lays claim to holding the one, universal, and unarguable truth is bound to alienate those who hold different truths. This is so obvious that only blindness can shield us from it.

There is a practical side as well. Holding together the balance of power has required and will require the maintenance of foreign bases and facilities. That in turn will call for the willing cooperation of other nations. Mere swashbuckling is unlikely to gain their consent.

CHAPTER 8

Dealing With Autonomous Major Powers

There are countries whose paths differ markedly from ours but which are too large and too consequential on the world scene for us to ignore. Russia and China are the chief examples. Russian history is replete with collapses of internal authority, leading to despotism. Today that infirmity seems to be in check, but there are frailties in its economy and its governance. China is now facing generational change in its ruling class, which may or may not lower its resistance to outside cultures. Both countries have vast military establishments, with nuclear weapon components, and a history of feeling themselves abused by the West.

Russia

Broadly speaking, Russia since 1990 has found itself in the midst of severe economic and political difficulties for which it must accept the principal responsibility, but for which the U.S. and the West have managed—unnecessarily—to attract a good part of the blame. Given the nuclear armaments, or "loose nukes," in Russia, it would be irresponsible for the West to walk away; but it is important for us to find the right mode of cooperation.

In the 1990s public and private international bankers saw it as their task to build a Western-style "market democracy" in Russia as an all-purpose cure for its post-Cold War ills. But the preconditions for liberal institutions were not in place. Key economic attributes, like capital markets and ease of entry, have never existed. Likewise, the political elements of a free system are missing: checks and balances, a federal system, a guaranteed free press, an independent judiciary. There is no bill of rights, and no effective limit on executive rule.

All this was well known before the fact. A leading authority on Russian politics, Seweryn Bialer at Columbia University, wrote in the 1980s that "the Western democratic model is not the birthright of every nation or society, nor is it the natural state of all societies. The odds of a Western-style democracy developing in an immense, multi-national country that has never in its entire history known a single day of political democracy are very long."

The Russian response to its liberation was first to abandon order, under Boris Yeltsin, and then to grasp it under his successor Vladimir Putin. There are some who fear this presages a return to Communist-style dictatorship. But not Mikhail Gorbachev, the leader who orchestrated an end to Communist control.

His colleague today in building a social democratic party, Aleksandr Gelman, has stated their shared view that Mr. Putin is seeking a proper balance for his country between freedom and order: "Russia is made in such a way that it either had a very strict discipline or it was anarchy."

In America our system can be summed up, as it once was by Justice Benjamin Cardozo, as an expression of "ordered liberty." In Russia, with its very different history and culture, the aim is more nearly "liberated order."

The key determinant here, as described in a 1990 assessment, is what scholars call political culture: "the sum of values and habits and expectations that shape a nation's institutions. . . . Human rights and democratic practices and entrepreneurial initiative are the flowers in this process, not the soil; they will blossom only after, and as a result of, the transformation of the culture."

Religion is a pertinent factor, and a divisive one. Russians traditionally see themselves as a chosen people of God, with Moscow as a "third Rome." They are the civilizers, the godly force. Market democracy has been something to oppose, not embrace, as a debasement of the ideals of community and spirituality. This is not simply a political perspective but a cultural one: It has been shared by such figures as Chekov, Solzhenytsin and Pope John Paul II (a fellow Slav).

The U.S. tendency, by contrast, has been to wield market democracy and advance it as a sort of instrumental religion. We prefer to ignore mixed models, like those of Sweden and Singapore, and to disregard as well our own heritage of a mixed economy with elements of state control and private enterprise side by side. We have fostered, in short, a conflict of values that is both unnecessary and ineffectual.

This is not a matter, again, of "walking away" from the Western heritage but of appreciating the longer time it may take for the Russians to come to terms with such shaping forces as the Renaissance, the Reformation and the Enlightenment—none of which they have ever experienced as a society. It is time to put aside divisive ideologies and to set realistic conditions that will allow us to contribute usefully to Russia's rebuilding.

China

Modern China, with the self-confidence to engage in market-opening reforms, also exhibited in the 1980s a certain openness to American strengths and purposes. This receptivity has been shut down more recently, however, in response to what the Chinese people as well as leaders perceive as U.S. provocations. These have intensified the movement of the leadership toward rigid internal Communist Party control.

In 2002, more than half of the ruling circle in China is slated for replacement. This will introduce a younger, more pragmatic generation but also one that has had little experience of the outside world.

Traditionally, the Chinese have had reason to be wary of that world—particularly of its religious component. In the 19th and early 20th centuries, there were four major uprisings against Chinese authority, sparked by Christian or Muslim or Buddhist elements. By the time the Maoists took power in the mid-1900s, contact with the West was seen as invariably contaminating. This helps to explain why Western religions to this day are kept under strict supervision, and why the Falun Gong, a seemingly harmless health sect, is repressed.

In the 1990s the U.S. showed remarkable insensitivity to Chinese fears. We thwarted the Chinese desire to host the Olympics, held up China's application to the World Trade Organization, abandoned our declared policy against high-level visits from Taiwan, and even bombed the Chinese embassy in Belgrade (which they could not believe was accidental). These events have succeeded in alienating the very youth, educated and modern, that we thought had aligned themselves with us after Tiananmen Square.

The clash of hypersensitivity and insensitivity was on full display after the collision of a U.S. surveillance plane with a Chinese pursuit jet off the southern coast of China in April 2001. The Chinese over-reacted from our point of view, and we underreacted from theirs. The U.S. claim, that the spying was "routine" and fully justified by international law, had no chance of bridging the difference. Fortunately, a longer-range view was taken by both parties and a joint process was established to try and civilize such encounters.

Recovering the lost ground will not require the abandonment of U.S. strength or firmness, which the Chinese know we have and expect us to exercise. It will require the use of tact and diplomacy, which have been so conspicuous by their absence. We need to become aware in particular that a stable and healthy China is in our interest. Asians in general believe that Chinese cohesion will help secure a balance in the region.

We in America need especially to disabuse ourselves of the notion that anything we do or say can serve to change China, or that we can force its government to yield to our prescriptions. Scholars of the region largely agree that this is not going to happen. What we should do instead is develop a positive agenda toward China, by which their interests and ours can find common ground or shared restraint as circumstances warrant.

Priorities

Policy depends on priorities. To be true to itself and its place in the world, America must pick a set of authentic foreign policy objectives and concentrate its resources on them, without undue distraction from lesser annoyances. That is how we can be effective, and also restrain ourselves from playing God.

In April 2000, the future National Security Adviser Condoleezza Rice spoke to this theme at the Woodrow Wilson Center for International Scholars. As capsuled in the Center's publication, *Link*, she said:

> The United States must stay focused on ensuring that relations with key countries of the world—such as Russia, China, and India—are thoroughly well managed. Too much time in the last decade has been spent dissipating U.S. resources on areas that are important for humanitarian reasons but that have dubious impact on U.S. national interests.

Discounting for campaign position, this points a direction that seems worth following.

Chapter 9

Engaging Volatile "Rogue" Nations

Success vs. Failure

The problem of dissipation is illustrated by what happened after "Desert Storm"—the U.S.-led rout of Iraqi forces that had overrun Kuwait. That was in all respects a focused campaign, drawing together a coalition of Arab and European and other nations and coordinating a sweeping victory that spelled denial to external aggression. Yet almost immediately there were complaints that the campaign had fallen short, that it should have pressed on to Baghdad and the eviction of Iraq's leader, Saddam Hussein.

There was no basis in the coalition consensus for taking such a step. The agreed aim had been to roll back conquest, and nothing more. The occupation of Baghdad would have entailed an entirely different mission, difficult to sustain, and splintering to the coalition. Nonetheless the legend has persisted that the U.S. missed a chance.

To cement the victory, the commanders in the field negotiated a set of agreements with the Iraqis calling for the abandonment of Iraq's missile program and its forsaking of development of weapons of mass destruction. The enforcement of these goals has been another matter. The U.S., with its chief ally the U.K., has tried bombing, inspection, and threatened removal of Saddam from power. None of these has worked. Nor has a regime of economic sanctions, which have successfully been portrayed as impacting the poor rather than the powerful. Today the Desert Storm coalition is largely in tatters, the Arab League estranged. Victory has been turned into victimization, and Saddam is calling the turn.

This has not been satisfying to the triumphalists in America, whose view is that U.S. policy should concentrate on getting rid of Saddam. The so-called Iraqi opposition, however, has no standing in that country and our financing of their meetings has led nowhere. Also, no one seems to ask whether a replacement figure in Iraq would be any improvement; whether, that is, conditions might actually worsen internally or in the region. These are basic questions.

The new Secretary of State, Colin Powell—who chaired the Joint Chiefs at the time of Desert Storm—has tried to turn things around. He has proposed tightening import controls and limiting them to armaments as a way of reestablishing leverage and beginning to knit the coalition back together again. It remains to be seen how far our politics may bend to this modest approach.

Diplomacy with "Rogues"

Terminologies may come and go, but attitudes persist. The U.S. treats troublesome governments as miscreants, or "rogues," and thereby makes it difficult to conduct diplomacy with them. This can defeat our ends. Robert S. Litwak, of the Wilson Center, has written trenchantly on the point:

> Although the term ["rogue"] ostensibly refers to violations of accepted international norms, it is a label that has no formal standing in international law. It derives instead from an American political culture that has traditionally viewed international relations as a clash between the forces of good and evil.
>
> But this approach, and the label itself, sharply limit diplomatic flexibility. It pushes policy makers into a one-size-fits-all strategy. Once a state, such as Iran, is declared beyond the pale and relegated to the rogue category, it is politically difficult to pursue an alternative approach.

Iran: Relations with this pivotal Middle Eastern state have been in a condition of stalemated antagonism since the seizure of American diplomatic hostages in Teheran in 1979. (For the Iranians, the formative offense was the CIA-driven overthrow of Premier Mossadegh in 1953, sometimes called "the hijacking of a nation.") Ambassador Bruce Laingen, the senior American hostage, promptly forgave his captors and has spent the ensuing 20 years working for restoration of relations. In his 1981 book, *Yellow Ribbon*, Laingen wrote that America's wish for Iran should be simply that it retain its independence of thought and action, using internal

processes of its own choosing. Whatever else the Khomeini revolution may signify, it has met that standard.

In Iran at present, the topmost religious leadership does not want a dialogue with the United States. But the elected political leadership does want that, and has made conciliatory overtures to which we have offered only grudging responses. Bruised pride is the obstacle on both sides, which is a condition familiar to religious counselors.

That condition will not suffice for dealings with a country that knows how to stunt our objectives. In March 2001, President Khatami concluded an arms deal with Russian President Putin, serving notice that these two nations at least intend to limit America's influence in the Middle East.

The United States natively has the self-confidence to reach out toward Iran with understanding and restraint, inviting reciprocity and overlooking momentary provocations. That seems the way to open ourselves to God and history.

North Korea: The Litwak article also spoke to relations with this nation:

> To mobilize support for its national missile defense policy, [the Clinton administration] has returned to calling North Korea a "rogue state." The use of the charged term has undercut the administration's ability to conduct further talks with the North Koreans or pursue a strategy that deviates from comprehensive containment or isolation.

To show the nonpartisan character of this trait, the new Bush administration decided as an early order of business that it too would refrain from immediate, follow-up negotiations.

But the problem North Korea presents is a pressing one. It is a starving nation with a bedraggled economy that has used a nuclear build-up to try and draw one or more major powers to step in as substitute patrons after the withdrawal of Russia from that role. It has a real need, above and beyond the recklessness of its nuclear behavior.

The U.S. responded with uncommon adroitness in 1994. It agreed to supply North Korean energy needs, in exchange for a verifiable suspension of its nuclear threat. In the process, South Korea, Japan, and China—the states most concerned—were extensively consulted, along with European powers. In this country there was a joinder of military, intelligence, and scholarly perspectives, making for a broad and workable consensus. The agreement has held up, although without some sort of follow-on arrangement it could wither or fold.

The chief proponent of pressing forward is Kim Dae Jong of South Korea, whose "sunshine policy" toward the North won him the Nobel Peace Prize. His critics in this country think Kim should not be allowed to set the pace; after all, the U.S. has kept substantial forces in Korea for nearly half a century. They want to be assured that diplomacy will produce real, verifiable results and that firmness will not be undercut by compassion. Above all, they want to avoid letting the U.S. be deceived by an unreliable North.

Such reservations are understandable but they are also too blunt. An exploration of the negotiating dynamics between the U.S. and North Korea would find that each must sort out competing values within its own culture. For Washington, the choice is between hope and skepticism; for Pyongyang, between autonomy and dependence. These are not simple equations.

To make or sustain progress, the U.S. will have to set clear limits on North Korean provocation but also attend remedially to that country's hardships. In a sense, we must equip ourselves to deal with an insecure and dysfunctional family member, using qualities of both firmness and restraint. It is a temptation, instead, to try and isolate the miscreant, but it does not work: Fidel Castro has survived such treatment for over 40 years.

What is needed most of all is statesmanship, not politics—a willingness to take the long view and embrace all pertinent concerns.

Non-State Actors

There are other volatile players, or rogues, in the field—individuals and syndicates with the power to wreak damage on our society. As with some state actors, the United States has been drawn to make popular but ill-advised and ultimately ineffective replies to their menace.

Terrorism: Muslims enlisted by the Taliban in the struggle for Afghanistan include people who say they have "consecrated their lives to jihad," as they understand that concept. These recruits have gone to killing school, seeing nothing irreligious in that indoctrination.

According to CIA estimates, trainees for this purpose have come from as many as 55 countries.

Others of comparably high-pitched ideological bent have gone after U.S. targets, including embassies and other prominent buildings. A number have been caught, others have not. The best known is Osama bin Laden, a wealthy Saudi Arabian who is thought to control networks of agents all over the world.

The question is, what tactics should be used in most cases to hunt down these figures and hold them to account? The U.S. has tried two approaches, the first of which has largely failed. That is to make a high-level, political affair out of our response, creating for example an "Office of Transnational Threats" in the National Security Council and directing a flawed missile attack against the presumed premises of the terrorists. This tends to play into their hands, giving the terrorists the publicity they seek and making martyrs of them.

More effective to date has been professional police and judicial cooperation among potential hide-out states, such as Canada, Britain, France, and Germany. Modest initiatives of this sort have paid real dividends.

Drug Wars: The wreckage of America's drug-strewn landscape is widely known and much lamented. Not so well known, until the recent film "Traffic," has been the misdirection of our efforts to combat the plague.

The predominantly military campaign to suppress foreign-source narcotics has cost this country many billions of dollars, but the supplies of such drugs have continued to soar. The latest enterprise, a $1.3 billion program for Colombia, is widely expected to have no impact on the drug trade while engaging us on the side of right-wing paramilitary forces that can only discredit the U.S. in the region.

There is a more effective alternative: drug treatment and education in this country. That was the course taken, successfully, by the Nixon administration. Its simple logic was that curtailing demand is bound to drive down supply. By the1980s, however, it became politically unfashionable to attend to drug users, and the public-health emphasis was abandoned.

The result is that a chiefly penal approach now prevails. It has created a prison population in this country larger than that of any other country, including Russia and China. That, and our routine resort to capital punishment, are major causes of disaffection with the United States in Europe and elsewhere.

Neither serpent nor dove would favor such misdirection.

— Chapter 10 —

Intervention in States of Internal Misrule

We move now from external to internal aggravations, from repelling invasions across boundaries to dealing with governments that mistreat their own nationals. There is a recognized difference in international law between the two cases: Traditionally, external aggression may be met with force but internal upsets are supposed to be left alone. And while publicists make the case for overriding the distinction, among major states there is still a reluctance to intrude, and a record of failure when this caution is forgotten.

As we have seen, the underlying difference is between protecting vital interests on the one side, and assuaging offended sensibilities on the other. We might prefer all rulers to behave in accordance with our ideas, but it is really not our business and if we make it so we are likely to be trespassing onto God's domain. In such cases history suggests that the proper posture is detachment, which is not the same thing as isolation. Indeed, detachment can forestall isolationism by avoiding the

54

unrealized moralism—and associated frustration—that followed Woodrow Wilson's efforts to rewrite human relations.

Our focus here again is on internal disarrays within foreign countries or regions that do not threaten the security interests of the United States; in recent years, these have included disturbances in Somalia, Haiti, Bosnia, and Kosovo. Their internal conduct has caused distress more to our sentiments than to our lives or fortunes. On the other side of that line, and warranting a forceful response, are such instances of aggression as World War II and the Persian Gulf War. Nothing in our analysis would call those engagements into question, just as nothing would rule out interventions freely invited by a nation state.

Theologically speaking, the question for our nation is whether and to what extent the internal reform of other states is an American prerogative. Modesty invites admission that there has been no sign of such a mandate. We must look now at a few particulars.

Military action

The first impulse in recent interventions has been to send in the troops—but not very far. Our leaders have felt politically constrained not to put the lives of American soldiers very much at risk, or at all if that can be managed. They have flown, for example, bombing runs over Kosovo at high altitude, which has spared the lives of the flight crews but has also avoided damage to targets on the ground. There is a tacit admission here, by our leaders, that the goals they pursue are not worth very much in the way of risk or sacrifice. That is close to admitting that the missions themselves are questionable.

One question is whose forces should intercede—if not American or NATO units, should it be the UN or somebody else? The UN record to date in such cases has been spotty, with problems of coordination and chain of command. There are proposals to create a standing volunteer army, with troops seconded to the UN from member states, but permanent Security Council members including the United States have been loath to delegate that much authority. There matters currently stand.

There is an intriguing alternative, which is to charge the middle-sized nations with the task of mounting interventions under their own command. General Lewis MacKenzie, a Canadian who led UN troops in Bosnia, has offered this as a preferable alternative to U.S. or UN or disorganized small-country peacemakers. Among its suggested merits is that it would free the United States to occupy itself with major, balance-of-power responsibilities that only it can handle.

But that still leaves the question whether or when any military response is appropriate. One of the striking facts that has emerged from this debate is the resistance to such ventures by senior military officers. Their junior officers like the idea of doing good works, of being useful, but the commanders doubt that this is what the forces were created to do. The accomplishments generally have not been as advertised, and the forces have as a rule been unable to finish their assignment and depart in the time allotted.

It was to get around such limitations that the "Powell Doctrine"—named for then Joint Chiefs Chairman, now Secretary of State, Colin Powell—was devised. This says, in its simplest form, that we should intervene militarily only when we are prepared to use overwhelming force and to win decisively in a brief time period. The doctrine was applied, successfully, in the Persian Gulf War. The problem is that internal misrule, as opposed to the external aggression at issue in that case, does not stir up the popular dismay that would justify an overwhelming military action. The Powell Doctrine in effect rules out military intervention in such cases.

Powell himself knew this. His admonition rose not just from military but from political reservations. In his autobiography, *An American Journey*, Powell wrote that he was following in the footsteps of General, later President, Dwight D. Eisenhower. "Eisenhower," he said, was a "war hero who did not have to bark or rattle sabers to gain respect and exercise command, a president who did not stampede his nation into every trouble spot, a man who understood both the use of power and the value of restraint and who had the secure character to exercise whichever was appropriate."

An inner strength, of course, along with an outward forbearance, are signs of a religious disposition.

Economic Sanctions

In lieu of military risk-taking, American political leaders have resorted more and more in recent years to the threat or use of economic warfare, imposing embargoes on a target country's trade or investment or financial activities. The efforts have mainly failed and even boomeranged, but our leaders have not found it convenient to admit defeat, and so the measures have lingered painfully and ineffectually on. It has not been a proud chapter in America's foreign policy.

The reasons for failure are not hard to find. Briefly put, sanctions of a social-policy character do not work well and they should not be expected to work. Their economics are typically weak, and their politics are counterproductive. Since they impose on what are seen as sovereign prerogatives, they stir up pride and prestige which serve to block any chance of diplomatic compromise. The weak and the innocent in the target state are the ones most hurt by the sanctions, while the wealthy and powerful can find ways of averting the sting. As privation grows among the less fortunate, they are drawn paradoxically closer to their domestic oppressors, both blaming the source of the sanctions for their ordeals.

There is to be sure an exception to this litany: South Africa, where over time a major change in the social policy of *apartheid* was brought about with the aid of external sanctions. The main leverage, however, was applied by the moral opposition within South Africa, whose leaders called for the imposition of sanctions as a sign of global solidarity. This meant that the ensuing suffering could not be exploited by the government of the day. It was as if a platoon leader, in combat, had called down friendly fire on his own position to dislodge a close-in enemy.

Nothing like that is available in most social-policy

disputes. In places like Iraq, and Haiti, there has been no effective internal opposition and therefore no one with whom an outsider could forge a working alliance. Instead, what has been created is a "rally round the flag" effect, building up the ruler's authority.

The modern champion of sanctions, Woodrow Wilson, did not foresee these difficulties. In his effort to persuade Americans of the value of the League of Nations, he argued strenuously for the worth of sanctions as an instrument of the League:

> Apply this economic, peaceful, silent, deadly remedy.
> . . . It does not cost a life outside the nation boycotted,
> but it brings pressure upon the nation which, in my judg-
> ment, no modern nation could resist.

How a remedy could be both "deadly" and "peaceful" does not appear. Limiting the moral compass to losses incurred by the boycotting state was unacceptable even at the time to Wilson's fellow Presbyterian, John Foster Dulles, who opposed sanctions on the ground that they would inevitably harm foreign innocents. Dulles proposed confining sanctions to arms embargoes and other measures that could afflict target leaders without imposing undue hardships on others.

That is the very shift that Secretary Colin Powell, against domestic opposition, is now trying to engineer in the sanctions against Iraq.

Iraq is a good example of another problem with sanctions, which is that they are forceful only if they are multilateral, but the coalition that joins in them is very hard to hold together. Suspicions arise of sanction-busting for economic advantage among the partners, followed soon after by the reality of disintegration. In Iraq, at present, goods on the embargo list now regularly arrive at its ports.

President George W. Bush, at his first White House news conference, admitted the difficulties and stated that "a good sanctions policy is one where the United States is able to build a coalition around the strategy." To that end, Secretary Powell was seen consulting with members of the Arab League, with the UN Secretary General, and with the four other permanent members of the Security Council. He faced additional resistance, however, from his own Congress; and whatever policy emerged would have to find a way around the generally dismal performance of sanctions.

Refugee Flows

One justification for intrusion into internal disruptions is that they sometimes cause massive dislocations of affected populations, which neighboring countries must then labor to accommodate. And indeed tens of millions of people, worldwide, are now said to be on the move because of domestic oppression, with many more displaced within their own countries. The whole sorry spectacle of "ethnic cleansing," in Bosnia and Kosovo, is an instance of this pressure. Also it is true that adjacent countries, particularly in poorer regions, find it hard to absorb large refugee migrations.

For such reasons the threat of mass migration has been made a basis for military intervention. The northern no-fly zone in Iraq was established by the U.S.-led coalition to prevent a migrant Kurdish population from upsetting the ethnic balance in adjoining Turkey, Russia and Iran. In Haiti, a large U.S. armada was assembled to retard refugee movements into Florida. And in Kosovo the displacement of Albanian populations was high among the causes of Western intervention.

But it is also the case that intervention can provoke the very refugee movements they aim to staunch. In Kosovo, no serious out-migration occurred until after the NATO bombing began. Economic sanctions, for their part, by worsening material conditions in places like Cuba and Haiti, tend to exacerbate the pressure to emigrate. The $1.3 billion aid package to Colombia, by bringing vast amounts of money into the reach of armed militias, is expected to drive fearful citizens toward the United States. So a refugee-based policy of intervention is at best quirky in its effects.

U.S. refugee policy itself is also inconsistent. Together with our major allies, our hospitality toward exile peoples shifted after the Cold War to a posture of exclusion, keeping the outflows bottled up at home. This is aimed quite openly at avoiding human "flooding" in the richer countries. The West has effectively turned its back on the "right to leave" earlier proclaimed in the Universal Declaration of Human Rights (1948) and the Helsinki Accords—each adopted in the flush of rivalry with the now-defunct Soviet Union.

So as a matter of declared policy the U.S. and the West are not prepared to remedy the dislocations that they themselves may produce by their interventions in other countries' domestic disturbances. Forcing refugees back into homes that have been destroyed or occupied by adversaries is not a formula for peace.

Yet the picture is more complicated than that. Strenuous ethnic lobbying in Washington has produced preferential refugee status for Cubans and former Soviet Jews and evangelical Christians. They can get in while others are kept out. That can be disturbing, for those who favor an even-handed rule of law. Still, it does not alter the relationship of immigration to intervention policy overall. The last places Americans today are going to try coercive interventions—short of an improbable, all-out war—are Russia and Cuba. Elsewhere the prospect of major, intervention-produced refugee migrations ought to be a deterrent to intrusion more than an invitation to it.

The Overall Record

It is remarkable how little public attention has been given to comparing the achievements of internal intervention with their declared goals. The fact is that, by this calculation, there have been almost no gains and a virtually unbroken string of failures.

Kosovo achieved none of the goals assigned to the NATO exercise by President Clinton. Serbian aggression was succeeded by Albanian aggression in a hostility that has now spread to Macedonia and, according to strategists, could engage our allies Greece and Turkey.

Bosnia has not attained the ethnic harmony projected for it by the Dayton agreement, and there is no prospect (if there ever was) that it will do so. On a broader front, while U.S. pundits and politicians were quick to claim credit for the eventual overthrow of the Milosevic regime in what remains of Yugoslavia, the victors in that

October 2000 election saw things differently. The new president, Vojislav Kostunica, declared that the U.S., as principal guarantor of the Dayton balance, had "kept Mr. Milosevic in power much longer than necessary." Kostunica has in consequence held the U.S. at arm's length.

Haiti has had no meaningful elections or relief from hardship. Crushing illiteracy and unemployment continue, as it was clear they would, to bar true democratic or free-market participation by the people.

Somalia has been listed by the UN World Food Program as having the highest percentage of undernourished people, a full 73 percent, of anyplace in the world. It was to redress hunger and malnutrition that the U.S. organized its ill-starred intervention into that country in early 1993.

And then there is the moral accounting, which has also been left undone. Ineffectual measures, long continued, with penalties visited upon the innocent, are fundamentally in violation of Just War principles. General James P. McCarthy, who led the air war in Kosovo, became persuaded both that the principles had been disregarded and that senior politicians in this country need to have the same rigorous exposure to those principles that the military has schooled itself to receive.

The law should be a factor here as well, although the tendency in Washington is to use it as a *post hoc* justification rather than as an advance guide to proper action. A few upright lawyers, especially in Vietnam, have stood up against that trend, but there is room for more. In the Kosovo campaign, an informal poll was conducted of leading professors of international law, and not one could find any persuasive legal justification for that strike. This ought at some point to stimulate reflection.

Americans can claim, as we usually do, the best of intentions. But a proper morality, the "morality of consequences," will not allow that—particularly when the consequences are reasonably foreseeable as they have been in these cases. The Just War principles do not admit an excuse for good intentions.

There is a practical side here, too. America's interventionist urges have been too broad, its resources too narrow, and its political will too feeble. The result has been to gobble up money, manpower, and leadership time and attention to no fruitful end.

There remain those, of course, who think the humanitarian claim on such assets is an absolute that demands their expenditure no matter what the cost. We shall have to look next at this view.

— CHAPTER 11 —

Human Rights Agenda

Theory and Practice

In the present state of play, while humanitarian goals have been strongly declaimed, there has been no one equipped to apply the needed political wisdom to the choice of intervention or abstention in a given case. Instead what has governed is the "CNN factor," namely, how much TV attention is given to mistreatments in one place or the other. President Clinton decided on well-judged historical grounds that the Balkans were not a good place to intervene. But his judgment was overborne by graphic pictures of carnage in Sarajevo. That sort of susceptibility does not yield principled or even prudential bases for decision.

The authenticity of our human rights agenda is also called into question by occasions in which it has been falsely claimed to be the motivating factor for intervention. In Grenada, in the West Indies, the U.S. justification for going in was that U.S. citizens were being held hostage. On the day before our invasion, the Grenadian authorities offered to release them. Our government "lost" that message, and attacked.

Also of importance is the law of unintended consequences, which in humanitarian cases appears to be the rule and not the exception. We may, once again, have good intentions, but fail to work through the implications or simply lack the power to bend them our way. The U.S. record of forecasting outcomes, says Professor Paul Griffiths of the University of Illinois, has been abysmal.

More disturbing still is the evidence of lack of political interest, at the highest levels, in what those outcomes are. Lofty aims are presented, and then to all appearances forgotten; results are measured instead by rolling criteria, making the best of whatever circumstances exist at the moment. By all appearances, posturing in these matters is more prized than performance. Attention to the actual needs of the oppressed comes across as distinctly secondary.

As for grounding our actions in international law, not only have we shown a sweeping disregard for that law but we have seriously misstated it. The two charters most often cited in support of U.S. human-rights interventions—the Universal Declaration of Human Rights and the Helsinki Accords—explicitly state they are not enforceable obligations. One can point to them rhetorically and invite compliance, but coercing anyone in their name violates their terms.

Sacred vs. Sovereign

It is plain that people at large have developed a distaste for inhumane conduct wherever it appears; this includes genocide, ethnic cleansing and systematic torture. But how should one act in relation to that distaste? And what does religion have to do with it? The theologian Martin Marty's "Sightings" service, on the Internet, has addressed itself to these issues:

> We know that religion—specifically, religious pluralism—played no small role in the violence and warfare that rocked sixteenth and seventeenth century Europe. Skeptics of current interventionism [may rightly] remember that a great dividend of the Westphalian sovereignty scheme was the formation of the nation-state, now freed to regulate its domestic affairs without external interference.
>
> So when humanitarian responses entail the invasion of another nation, we might wonder whether religion is asking us to trespass against the cardinal premise and virtue of political sovereignty. In the end, is religion gesturing to reclaim sacred space from sovereign states?

To which we might answer that it depends what kind of "religion" one is looking at. A triumphal faith, or a condescending one, might rush across the borders and take its chances on the resurgence of bloody, holy war. A modest or a humble faith would probably not.

Also, if we are interested in matters of fundamental fairness, the Westphalian system exists today to protect weaker states against intrusion. The stronger ones can protect themselves, and there is no likelihood of a Western invasion of Russia or China even though we deprecate their treatments of Chechnyans and Tibetans. A system that picks on the weak in the name of justice is hard to perceive as an exercise of high principle.

Diversity of Values

Life might be simpler if all value systems were identical, but they are not. It might also be simpler if there were a clear hierarchy of religions, with "higher" and "lesser" belief structures, but this is also not the case. As the apostle Peter discovered with the centurion Cornelius, another's faith credentials may differ markedly from one's own and still provide food for thought.

Asians in particular tend to differentiate their values from those of the West. This stance meets resistance from partisans of universal human-rights enforcement, but there is truth to it. In a dialogue with Reinhold Niebuhr on the point many years ago, Hans Morgenthau (the realist) said:

> [The Asian view] is not an individualistic conception of dignity, but there is an approach to equality and to mutual aid that has its own high value. . . . We [Westerners] hope that China will find its own way to the spiritual and cultural freedom that is so precious to us, [but] it may take different institutional forms.

Child labor, for example, is anathema to us but in the economic and family patterns of many Eastern and Southern countries, it is a practice of solidarity.

Lee Kuan Yew, the legendary former prime minister of Singapore where free-market opportunities flourish in an authoritarian society, recently spoke to the theme of diversity:

> Immensely powerful forces of new technology are sweeping the world. . . . To compete, we need a change of mind-set to encourage innovation and creativity. [But] there is no reason to abandon our values.

Confucianism must adjust and change with changing structures of the economy and society. [Yet] it is not necessary to be disrespectful. The basic human relationships [including that] between a citizen and his government . . . do not change. They have made for order and civility.

It's different from Western individualism, where the individual is glorified as the freewheeling, unrestrained creative agent of progress. This has not been the ideal in Asia, and the Internet won't change that.

There are those who say that the Internet will flood Asia with democratic ideas. Does it follow that these American ideas and practices will take root in Asian societies that have different histories and cultures?

. . . . Democracy needs more than freedom of the press and freedom of association. The necessary preconditions are near-universal education and a large middle class.

For some years now, the U.S. Department of State has produced an annual rating of human-rights practices in countries around the world, using Western values as a standard. The Chinese have finally had enough of it, and have issued their own counter-report, "U.S. Human Rights Record in 2000." It details, for example, our large number of deaths by gunfire, the role of big money in our election campaigns, and the unrivaled size of our prison populations. We might have said the same things ourselves.

Evolution, Not Revolution

Those who question the universality of American views on these matters tend to have history on their side.

Robert D. Kaplan, the author of the Balkan history that kept Clinton for a time out of that region, later wrote:

> [D]emocracy emerges successfully only as a capstone to other social and economic achievements. In his "author's introduction" to Democracy in America, Tocqueville showed how democracy evolved in the West not through the kind of moral fiat we are trying to impose throughout the world but as an organic outgrowth of development.

> . . . . Our often moralistic attempts to impose Western parliamentary systems on other countries are not dissimilar to the attempts of nineteenth century Western colonialists—many of whom were equally idealistic—to replace well-functioning chieftancy and tribal patronage systems with foreign administrative practices.

Hence the NPR epithet, previously given: "Liberal Humanitarian Imperialism."

Back in the heyday of imperialism, there were those who saw and opposed. One such was the English historian and statesman Thomas Babington Macaulay. Rising in the House of Commons in 1845 to oppose an economic penalty on Brazilian sugar grown with the help of slave labor, Macaulay said:

> No independent nation will endure to be told by another nation, "We are more virtuous than you; we have sat in judgment on your institutions; we find them to be bad; and as a punishment for your offenses, we condemn you to pay higher duties at our Customs House than we demand from the rest of the world."

Perhaps the strongest historical precedent is that of our own Civil War. It was fought in places with brutal inhumanity. And yet the British, who sympathized with the South, did not intervene, and neither did anyone else. Who is to say that the eventual settling of regional antipathies in this country, and even the softening of racial hostility, did not benefit from our being left to our own devices? And if this worked for us, why might it not work—again, after time and travail—for the Balkans or Central Africa?

The story is told of a boy who discovered a cocoon writhing with the exertions of an emerging butterfly. Sympathizing, he reached in to help. Sadly, the insect drooped and expired because it had not been given the chance to build its own strengths.

Counsel of Elders

A final word can be given to the venerated diplomatic historian, now approaching his centenary, Ambassador George F. Kennan:

> What we ought to do at this point is to try to cut ourselves down to size in the dreams and aspirations we direct to our responsibilities for world leadership. . . . This whole tendency to see ourselves as the center of political enlightenment and as teachers to a great part of the rest of the world strikes me as unthought-through, vainglorious and undesirable. . . . I would urge a far greater detachment, on our government's part, from other nations' domestic affairs.

CHAPTER 12

Judicializing Intervention

International Criminal Court

In an effort to muffle the accusations of imperialism, the U.S. and the West have sponsored war-crimes tribunals in some of the areas of upheaval, notably (former) Yugoslavia and Rwanda. These have encountered various limitations, so American diplomats took the lead in proposing an International Criminal Court of general jurisdiction, to sit at The Hague. That initiative was scuttled by the Clinton administration, on the ground of prosecutorial risk to U.S. peace-keeping forces. (No one appears to have noticed the asymmetry of obligation, or taint of "victor's justice," associated with this stated cause for withdrawal.)

At all events the Court seems certain to be approved by a sufficient number of other nations, which means that it should be useful to address its other deficiencies.

To begin with, the Nuremberg war-crimes precedent does not really apply. It arose out of a World War II context of "unconditional surrender" with outside occupation and governance—none of which is present in current-day humanitarian interventions. When countries continue to govern themselves, the cooperation of their authorities is required for domestic tranquility, and is not to be obtained by criminal prosecution.

In today's environment, the trial of offenders has been mainly limited to minor figures. This does not carry much weight, but it is what has been brought to the bar of the courts considering international crime. The capture and trial of major figures has proven to be problematic or undesirable or both. That is likely to be the case with the new Court as well.

There is, moreover, a looseness to the definition of human-rights offenses, starting with a vague description of genocide, and widening as it reaches aggression and crimes against humanity for which there are no agreed definitions at all. This is a product of undue ambition on the part of the academic drafters of the authorizing treaty. They were offered, but rejected, an opportunity to limit the mandatory jurisdiction of the Court to cases of well-defined genocide, and to leave broader offenses to voluntary submission. By seeking to run before they could walk, they appear to have done in the venture.

Political Judgment

Beyond these points of legal infirmity, there is a basic question about the wisdom of shifting from politics to law in dealing with humanitarian conflicts. The highly astute Polish architect of the Solidarity movement, Adam Michnic, has said that "the greatest political innovation of the late 20th century is the negotiated end to repressive or military regimes." Threatening those regimes with prosecution would, instead, entrench them in office.

A test case was the attempted arrest and trial of the Chilean dictator Augusto Pinochet. Indicted in Spain and detained in England, Pinochet was ruled liable for oppression although let go on medical grounds. Michnic, whose liberal and humanitarian credentials cannot be questioned, came out strongly against this judicial assertion of authority:

> Pinochet has in his country many supporters, to whom the general's trial would amount to a breaking of the internal consensus. The Spaniards should recall the reasons why they decided to forego a settling of the accounts for the victims of the Franco dictatorship. . . . [Y]ou have to choose between the logic of reconciliation and the logic of justice. Pure justice leads to new civil war. I prefer the negotiated revolution.

Revolution, by itself, requires the scrambling of eggs. Reconciliation entails their careful separation. Criminal prosecution appears too blunt an instrument for that assignment.

Alternative Measures

In countries around the world that are now recovering from oppression, there is an interesting if uneven movement toward a domestic justice of restoration rather than retribution. This may be joined with negotiation processes to bring about a state of reconciliation. Nations where this has been taking place include South Africa, Cambodia, Argentina, perhaps Chile and even Serbia.

Key ingredients are admission of offenses, contrition, and restitution—although these may vary in application from place to place. The Arab *sulha* tradition provides, at village level, a working model for those interested. The work of the South African Truth and Reconciliation Commission, chaired by Nobel Peace Prize winner archbishop Desmond Tutu, has attracted wide attention.

Potential benefits of such an approach include: displacement of foreign by domestic tribunals; subjection of law to political purposes; assuaging deeply held resentments; and easing offenders out of office. Reinhold Niebuhr would probably have approved. In *An Interpretation of Christian Ethics*, he wrote:

> Forgiveness in the absolute sense is . . . an impossibility as much as any other portion of Christ's perfectionism. . . . Yet it is possible to qualify the spiritual pride of the usually self-righteous guardian of public morals [and] to engage in social struggles with a religious reservation in which lie the roots of the spirit of forgiveness.

Another supporter would have been Abraham Lincoln, whose second Inaugural Address at the close of the Civil War offered "malice toward none" and "charity for all"—despite the humanitarian horrors of the Confederacy's Andersonville prison, described as a "disgrace to civilization." Lincoln wanted to bind up the wounds of a shattered nation, and this was the course he chose.

— CHAPTER 13 —

Globalization

The world has been changing remarkably in the post-Cold War era, in ways that transcend settled boundaries and disturb settled cultures. The motive force comes primarily from travel and technology, particularly the technologies of information flow. The columnist Thomas Friedman paints the resulting dilemma for the smaller, more traditional societies:

> On the one hand, societies need to link up with the global economy and attract global investment in order to survive economically. But at the same time, the more societies ask their citizens to link up with distant, sterile economic structures—like GATT, NAFTA or the EU— the more they need to find ways to give their people the ability to express their distinctive cultural, religious and national identities. Countries are like people. They have bodies and souls, and both need to be nourished.

Among those who have felt spiritually ill-fed are the ayatollah caste in Iran, which threw out the shah because he had become too identified with modernization. Their upheaval shows the explosive force of cultural discontent if left unattended. And it also shows that the Western religion of "market democracy" may serve as a cause, more than a cure, for such disaffection.

The American Role

Anti-corporate globalization protest movements have been directed at international institutions of trade and investment, like the World Trade Organization, the World Bank, and the International Monetary Fund. But the dominant force behind those institutions, people notice, is the United States of America. We bring the bitter, as well as the better, in modernization; and we need to be careful not to attract all resentments toward ourselves.

There is an important positive side to what is happening, a set of healthy tremors if you will. The new dispensation, when allowed to, can work to unravel corruption, inefficiencies and despotism. That could bring a fair amount of good will our way. But this is not automatic. Much of the world is governed by authoritarian elites who shun modernization precisely because it would challenge their grip on power. Other leaders want the economic benefits but worry about the cultural stresses. It will take concentrated political insight and finesse to navigate these currents. And there are American businesses that could teach our government a thing or two about such qualities.

At present the problem is imperfectly understood in American politics. In his prepared confirmation testimony, Secretary of State-designate Colin Powell said that America and its allies can reshape the world by their simple willingness to trade openly and to invite their partners to do likewise. But Powell was also moved to say that the U.S. has "an interest in every place on earth; we need to lead, to guide, to help, in every country that has a desire to be free, open and prosperous." So long as we allow other countries to express that desire, and do not presume them into it by the force of our will, this may work out.

Foreign Assistance

U.S. and multilateral aid programs, such as they are, will have to be re-evaluated in the light of changing global demographics. The world is becoming less and less centered on the West. By the year 2050, according to UN projections, 60 percent of the world's population will reside in China, India and Africa alone—up from 40 percent at present. The advanced economies will retain their present populations, but in 2050 that will constitute only one-eighth of the total. Who, at that point, will represent the dominant culture?

To put the question plainly, will Westernization—or, for that matter, homogenization—represent an attainable ideal? An emerging perception is that societies will and should be free to select among cultural models, adopting what is helpful and sticking with what feels authentic. As this sense develops, it should help globalization become a force for variation rather than for uniformity.

That notion has yet to catch on among development officials in the West. There is instead a Procrustean template, called a "Washington consensus," of ten stated principles that are considered necessary to development. At the same time there are already alternatives, as manifested by the East Asian "tiger" states that have pursued market diversity side-by-side with political centralism.

In the face of these developments, and the population movements behind them, it seems evident that in future years the U.S. and the West will have to become more open and less unilateral in their modeling for the rest of the world.

Exporting Democracy

The United States at present is, however, still pushing Western-style democracy on countries that may or may not be prepared for it. Both public and semi-public agencies, like the National Endowment for Democracy (NED), have been authorized to aid election processes, work on government reform, and help build civil institutions, anywhere in the world.

Where this is invited, once again, no problem arises Former President Jimmy Carter has made one of his careers out of monitoring elections as an invitee. But very often there is no invitation, and all too often the U.S. intrusion is ham-fisted or ignorant or both. The result can be a setback to U.S. interests.

In Serbia, for example, opposition leaders were deeply embarrassed by a U.S.-drafted public summons to them to support the extradition of Slobodan Milosevic, who seized on the occasion to brand the opposition as a bunch of puppets. In Haiti, where 22,000 American soldiers were dispatched to "restore" a democracy that had never existed, five percent of the eligible voters took part in an ensuing election, and deep hardship and chronic instability remain. These are not the imprints of an effective policy.

Nor was the outcome of a grand Democracy Conference put together by the United States in June 2000. This gained, at best, the pained tolerance of our Western allies, while the British Foreign Minister stayed home. It produced a declaration itemizing the institutions of democracy: free and fair elections, the rule of law, freedom of religion and the press, freedom from arbitrary seizure, and freedom of association.

This essential replica of the U.S. Bill of Rights is not likely to travel very far. A checklist of desired institutions fails to capture the necessity for cultural transformation before any society is equipped to practice democracy. It cannot be considered a serious effort.

Robert D. Kaplan is just one of the scholar-diplomats who have criticized this kind of work. He writes:

> Those who think that America can establish democracy the world over should heed the words of the late American theologian and political philosopher Reinhold Niebuhr: "The same strength which has extended our power beyond a continent has also . . . brought us into a vast web of history in which other wills, running in oblique or contrasting directions to our own, inevitably hinder or contradict what we most fervently desire. We cannot simply have our way, not even when we believe our way to have the happiness of all mankind as its promise."

Likewise from Richard Haass, the newly named director of Policy Planning for Secretary of State Colin Powell:

> The positive vision of a world of liberal democracies living in harmony simply does not comport with a reality that is often anything but harmonious and in which many societies are and will remain less than completely

democratic. Promoting democracy and human rights may be important . . . but U.S. foreign policy can only rarely accomplish this.

And from outside our shores, the words of Kishore Mahbumani, former ambassador of Singapore to the United Nations:

> How does one successfully transplant democracies into societies that historically have had very different social and political systems? The conventional wisdom in some American political and intellectual circles today is that any society, including China, can make this transformation virtually immediately. Yet most Western societies (including the most recent cases, like Spain and Portugal) did not make the leap overnight from traditional or semi-feudal systems. . . . Earlier theorists of democracy would be surprised by the twentieth-century conceit that democracy can be applied to any society, regardless of its stage of development or its internal social divisions.

Finally, from within the Carnegie Endowment for International Peace, which has offered the most thoughtful support for democracy promotion, comes this restraining view:

> Democracy aid, as well as the complementary tools of diplomatic and economic carrots and sticks, can do little to change the fundamental social, economic, and political structures and conditions that shape political life in other countries. . . . Basing a call for a democracy-oriented foreign policy on an assumption of vast American influence over other countries' political fortunes only sets up the policy edifice for a fall.

Governments and their emissaries, to summarize, may be inherently unsuited to the task of transforming each other. Here if ever is a mission for God, and history. Serious thought should be given, accordingly, to repealing the NED legislation and deauthorizing the departments of government, apart from a clearly defined class of cases of foreign-state invitation.

— Chapter 14 —

The Primacy of Culture

Harvard Professor Lawrence Harrison, editor of the compendium, "Culture Matters," has summed up its major points as follows:

- Culture in the sense of underlying attitudes and practices is the principal conditioner of societies everywhere in the world.

- Cultures can and do change from within, but change cannot be imposed from without.

For, as was written by the present author a dozen years ago, "the key determinant is what scholars like to call political culture: the sum of values and habits and expectations that shape a nation's institutions. . . . Human rights and democratic practice and entrepreneurial initiative are the flowers in this process, not the soil; they will blossom only after, and as a result of, the transformation of the culture."

So, for example, Islamic societies may evolve toward a better accommodation with the West, but only by drawing on the strengths of their own traditions. There is for this purpose a difference between the nay-saying of fundamentalism and the yea-saying of revival. The latter, according to Professor Abdul Aziz Said, "combines a rediscovery of the vitality of the Islamic experience with a determination not to submit any longer to the cultural humiliation of judging oneself by Western standards." A like observation might be made about other developing cultures around the world.

The very terminology of "developed" and "developing" is itself culturally conditioned. It refers to relative *economic* standing. If the index were of artistic or spiritual achievement, the ratings might often be reversed.

"What is unreasonable," Robert D. Kaplan has noted, "is to put a gun to the head of the peoples of the [economically] developing world and say, in effect, 'Behave as if you had experienced the Western Enlightenment to the degree that Poland and the Czech Republic did.' " That is to force culture rather than accept it.

The proper attitude for us in this country is acceptance and humility. It is an attitude precisely contrary to the temerity that produced the International Religious Freedom Act of 1998. This statute established an "ambassador for religious freedom" and a supporting commission to monitor religious practices world-wide and recommend how to bring them into line with our preferences. It has given rise to all sorts of problems of definition. But the basic question is what business it is of ours to define and enforce religion anywhere. And how are we going to advance American interests around the world if we continue to do everything we can to alienate friends and supporters?

It is not just foreign cultures that are at issue, in the end, but our own. In a world where persuasiveness is at least as important as conviction, it is not clear that we can any longer afford our self-defeating impositions. Does America have to come a cropper, be upended by God and history, before we pay attention? The answer, for a people raised in a faithful relationship to divine authority, should certainly be no. All we need do, fundamentally, is return to the allegiances that shaped us at the birth of our American experiment.

Annexes

A. Forum Participants

(in Forum sessions, 1998-2001)

The Rev. Katharine Babson
Founder, Hanoi International School

Christina Bolton
Capitol Strategies

The Rev. Hugh Brown
Episcopal chaplain, Georgetown University

Muneer Choudhury
Presidential adviser, Bangladesh

The Rev. Drew Christiansen
Woodstock Theological Center

David Cohen
The Advocacy Institute

Donald Deline
Halliburton Company

Arthur Downey
Baker Hughes, Inc.

The Rev. Joseph Eldridge
Chaplain, American University

The Rev. Roy Enquist
Lutheran Seminary

The Rev. Alan Geyer
Ethicist, Washington Cathedral

Joseph Grimes
Legal analyst, ARD

Gail Harrison
Shandwick Public Affairs

Thomas Hart
Episcopal Church Office

Imam Yahya Hendi
Muslim chaplain, Georgetown University

The Rev. Marguerite Henninger
Christ Church, Georgetown

Roland Homet
Forum director

J. Leon Hooper, S.J.
Woodstock Center

Bradford Johnson
Institute of World Affairs

Dr. Robert Johnson
Former NSC staff

Douglas Johnston
Center for Religion & Diplomacy

The Rev. Thomas Laird Jones
Habitat for Humanity International

Lorelei Kelly
Congressional study group

Fr. John Langan
Kennedy Institute for Ethics

Ernest Lent
Episcopal Peace Commission

Hon. Samuel Lewis
Former U.S. ambassador to Israel

David Little
Harvard Divinity School

Hon. Alan Lukens
Former U.S. ambassador in Africa

Rodney MacAlister
Conoco, Inc.; Prayer Breakfast board

Gerard Powers
U.S. Catholic Conference

Prof. Abdul Aziz Said
Islamic Studies, American University

Therese Saint-Andre
Inter-American Development Bank

Dr. Tim Sedgwick
Virginia Theological Seminary

Rabbi Gerald Serotta
Chaplain, George Washington University

Meena Sharify-Funk
Islamic Studies, American University

Nancy Soukup
Watson Institute, Brown University

Peter Spalding
FSO and seminarian

Douglas Tanner
Faith and Politics Institute

Hashim el-Tinay
President, Salam Sudan

Corinne Whitlatch
Churches for Middle East Peace

Also in attendance:

Zarrin Caldwell
UN Association of the USA

Kevin Clements
Institute for Conflict Resolution

John Cullinan
U.S. Catholic Conference

Pamela Moffat
Jubilee 2000

Joseph Sills
UN Information Center

B. Forum Presenters

(by date)

Roland Homet, *Lawyer, diplomat, author*
"The Forgotten Virtues of Diplomatic Detachment"   March 1998

Fr. John Langan, S.J., *Kennedy School of Ethics*
"The Place of Values in Foreign Affairs"   April 1998

Dr. David Little, *U.S. Institute of Peace*
"Restorative or Retributive Justice for H.R. Offenses"   May 1998

Amb. Jonathan Dean, *Union of Concerned Scientists*
"NATO Expansion: An Imbalance of Power?"   June 1998

Roland Homet, *Forum director*
"Premature Westernization of Mother Russia"   September 1998

Bishop Mark Dyer & Dr. Axel von Trostenburg,
Episcopal Seminary & World Bank
"Third World Debt Relief"   October 1998

Dr. George Irani, *Islamic scholar, American U.*
"Islamic Assertiveness"   November 1998

Dr. Larry Darby, *Information economist*
"Globalization and Its Discontents"   January 1999

Dr. Oswald Guinness, *Trinity Forum*
"American Experiment"   February 1999

Lt. Gen. Howard Graves, USA, *Former Commandant, West Point*
"U.S. Ideals and Interests Abroad"   March 1999

Senator Mary Landrieu (D.-La.), *Armed Services Committee*
"Role of the Church in Public Policy"   April 1999

Dr. Colin Bradford, *Ex-chief economist, USAID*
"Future Focus of Foreign Assistance" May 1999

Amb. Bruce Laingen, *Senior diplomatic hostage*
"Restoring Relations with Iran" June 1999

Roland Homet, *Forum director*
"Assessing Humanitarian Intervention" September 1999

Dr. Robert Dunn, *Economics professor, GWU*
"WTO Regulation of Labor and the Environment" October 1999

Bradley O. Babson,*World Bank analyst*
"The Delicate Diplomacy with North Korea" November 1999

Hon. Monroe Leigh, *International lawyer*
"The Proposed International Criminal Court" January 2000

Kathleen Newland, *Carnegie Endowment*
"Post-Cold War Refugee and Asylum Policy" February 2000

David Cohen, *Advocacy Institute*
"The Role of NGO's in International Relations" April 2000

Maj. Charles Pfaff, U.S. Army, *West Point faculty*
"Religion and Reconciliation in the Middle East" May 2000

Michael Massing, *Investigative journalist*
"Misadventures of the Drug War" June 2000

Thomas Carothers, *Lawyer, author*
"Promoting Democracy Abroad" September 2000

The Rev. Michael Hamilton, *Washington Cathedral*
"International Economic Challenges" October 2000

Douglas H. Paal, *China specialist*
"Encountering the New China" November 2000

C. Forum Documents

Note: *To access and download any document,
enter the Forum's website at <www.relpol.org>,
and click on "Papers"*

SUMMARIES

Diplomatic Detachment (outline)
Diplomatic Detachment (discussion)
Catholic Diplomacy
Restorative Justice
NATO Expansion
Westernizing Russia (outline)
Westernizing Russia (discussion)
Third World Debt
Islamic Assertiveness
Globalization
American Experiment
Ideals and Interests
Church in Public Policy
Future of Foreign Aid
Relations with Iran
Human Rights Agenda
World Trade Organization
North Korea Diplomacy
International Criminal Court
Refugee Policy
Role of NGO's
Religion in Middle East
Drug Wars

Democracy Promotion
International Economy
The New China
"Sacred and Sovereign"

READINGS

The New Realism
National Security
Sufi Perceptions
War Crimes
Protestant "Deformation"
Reconciliation
Islamic Traditions
NATO Expansion
Ideals and Interests
NATO Agenda
Forgiveness
Case for Modesty
Islam
Islam
Israel
Globalism
Religion and Foreign Policy
Hegemony

FORUM TOPICS IN THE NEWS

Tact / NATO Strategy
UN Conference on Religion
Realpolitik / War on Drugs
U.S. Example
Humanitarian Intervention

PASSING PARADE

Intervention
Detachment
Hegemony
Religion / Detachment
Democracy Promotion
NGO Roles
Hegemony / Globalism
Diplomatic Detachment
Balance of Powers
Democracy Promotion
Westernization
China and the West
Intervention / Religion
Holy War
Limits of Power
Hegemony
Intervention / Hypocrisy

D. Press Participants

(attendees at Forum-sponsored
breakfast meetings, 1999-2000)

Jim Anderson	Freelance
Ted Clark	National Public Radio
Norman Kempster	*Los Angeles Times*
Steven Mufson	*Washington Post*
Bill Nichols	*USA Today*
Jane Perlez	*New York Times*
Miles Pomper	*Congressional Quarterly*
Barry Schweid	Associated Press
Douglas Waller	*Time Magazine*
Charles Wolfson	CBS News
Jonathan Wright	Reuters News Service

E. Selected Bibliography

John C. Bennett & Harvey Seifert, *U.S. Foreign Policy and Christian Ethics* (1977)

Thomas Friedman, *From Beirut to Jerusalem* (1995 ed.)

Peter Gomes, *The Good Book* (1996)

Richard Haass, *The Reluctant Sheriff* (1997)

Roland Homet, *The New Realism* (1990)

Elias Jabhour, *Sulha* (1993)

Robert D. Kaplan, *The Coming Anarchy* (2000)

James Korth, "The Protestant Deformation and American Foreign Policy," in *Orbis* (Faith and Statecraft issue, Spring 1998)

Kishore Mahbumani, "The West and the Rest," in *The National Interest* (Summer 1992)

Walter McDougall, *Promised Land, Crusader State* (1997); "Introduction," in *Orbis* (Faith and Statecraft issue, Spring 1998)

Reinhold Niebuhr, *The Children of Light and the Children of Darkness* (1972)

Robert Osgood, *Ideals and Self-Interest in America's Foreign Relations* (1953)

A.Philip Parnham, *Letting God* (1987)

Abdul Aziz Said & Nathan C. Funk, *Islam and the West* (1998)

Emmanuel Sivan, "The Holy War Tradition in Islam," in *Orbis* (Faith and Statecraft issue, Spring 1998)

Symposium on "Forgiveness in Public Life," in *Church and Society* (May-June 1998)

Woodrow Wilson Center, *At the End of the American Century* (1998)

F. Notes to the Text

Unless otherwise specified, Biblical citations
are to the New Oxford Annotated Bible
(New Revised Standard Version, 1991)

Frontispiece

GENESIS: The usual translation, "knowledge of good and evil," can equally be rendered, "knowledge of all things." Good News Bible (1979), Genesis 2:9, note.

Chapter 1

AMERICAN CREED: See James Kurth, "The Protestant Deformation and American Foreign Policy," in *Orbis* (Faith and Statecraft issue), Spring 1998.

POLITICAL LIBERALS AND CONSERVATIVES ALIKE: On January 26, 2001, less than a week after his inauguration, President George W. Bush was handed a petition from a group of leading neoconservatives, arguing that "American leadership must never remain indifferent to tyranny, must never be agnostic about the virtues of political and economic freedom, must always be concerned with the fortunes of fragile democracies." *Washington Post*, January 27, 2001.

GANDHI: Quoted by Walter McDougall, "Introduction," in *Orbis* (Faith and Statecraft issue), Spring 1998.

"WILSONIAN NATION": Senator John McCain, debating in the South Carolina Republican primary on CNN, February 16, 2000.

Chapter 2

EMPIRES PAST AND PRESENT: R.W. Apple, Jr., *New York Times,* January 1, 2000; Henry Kissinger, *Washington Post,* January 10, 2000.

IMPERIAL CONDESCENSION: Robert Kagan and William Kristol, "A Superpower's Place in the Post-Cold War World," *Washington Post* Outlook section, March 19, 2000: "Given the dangers we know, and given the certainty that unknown perils await us over the horizon, there can be no respite from our burden of *benevolent, global hegemony.*"

MOTHER TERESA: Her counsel follows that of Jesus in Matthew 25:31-40: "Truly I tell you, just as you did [acts of charity] to one of the least of these who are members of my family, you did it to me."

EDEN AND BABEL: Genesis 3:1-5, 11:1-9.

BIBLICAL SCHOLARS: *A Theological Word Book of the Bible* (10th ed. 1978), p. 120.

GOOD INTENTIONS: They can lead us astray, "through self-deception, pride and moral ambition." Peter Gomes, *The Good Book* (1996).

SREBRENICA: UN Secretary General Kofi Annan, "Srebrenica Report," November 15, 1999.

KING BELSHAZZAR: "Mene, mene, tekel, parsin" (Daniel 5:25) can be read in English as "number, number, weight, divisions" (Good News Bible). The king was tested and found wanting: Israel Shamir, Russian Israeli journalist and translator (e-mail transmission).

ROBERT L. HUTCHINGS: *At the End of the American Century,* chapter 5 (Woodrow Wilson Center, 1998).

HEGEMONY AND ITS DISCONTENTS: See the excellent article by Josef Joffe, editor of the German weekly *Die Zeit*, in the *New York Times* for June 20, 2000.

AMERICA'S NEED FOR OVERSEAS PARTNERS: Detailed in a 1997 study by the RAND Corporation; security and spiritual needs here coincide.

POPE JOHN XXIII: Recounted by the former Catholic educator Paul Purta; the Latin is *omnia videre, multa dissimulare, pauca corrigere.*

AMERICAN AND EUROPEAN STATESMANSHIP: Roland Homet, *The New Realism* (1990).

WALTER McDOUGALL: "Introduction," in *Orbis* (Faith and Statecraft issue), Spring 1998.

1977 STUDY: John C. Bennett & Harvey Seifert, *U.S. Foreign Policy and Christian Ethics* (1977).

Chapter 3

SHARED ABRAHAMIC ORIGINS: Muslims trace their ancestry back to Abraham through Hagar's son Ishmael. Genesis 21:20 note.

EXCLUSION BY JEWS OF NON-JEWS: Ezra, chapters 9, 10. See also 1 Kings 11:1-13, portraying King Solomon's non-Jewish marriages which came to be seen as the provoking cause of the Exile of the Jews from Israel.

THE KAHANES: *Washington Post,* January 5, 2001.

COUNTER-CRUSADES: Emmanuel Sivan, "The Holy War Tradition in Islam," *Orbis* (Faith and Statecraft issue), Spring 1998.

BELEAGUERMENT: Eyad el-Sarraj, "Resist With Peace," *Washington Post*, March 31, 2001.

ONE-SIDED ISRAELI COMMENTARY: Israel Shamir, "Acid Test Failed," *RI* (*Russian Israeli Weekly*), December 27, 2000.

ISLAMIC FRUSTRATION: Abdul Aziz Said & Nathan C. Funk, *Islam and the West,* (CSIS, 1998); Fouad Adjani, "Where U.S. Power Is Beside the Point," *New York Times*, October 17, 2000. See also Susan Sachs, "Despair Beneath the Arab World's Rage," The New York Times, October 14, 2001; Dennis Overbye, "How Islam Won, and Lost, the Lead in Science," The New York Times, Science section, October 30, 2001

JEWISH MORAL STANDARDS: Thomas Friedman, *From Beirut to Jerusalem* (1995 ed.), pages 432-33, 450, 567.

"SILVER RULE": Favored by Jewish, Baptist, Jesuit, and Muslim clergy at a Kanuga (Episcopal) conference on Jerusalem in July 1998. The Golden Rule, more intrusively, says: "*Do* unto others . . ." Luke 6:30.

ISLAMIC PLURALISM: Said & Funk, *op. cit. supra.*

RESURGENCE OF ISLAMIC MODERATION: Genevieve Abdo, "How Moderate Islam Is Transforming Egypt," *Washington Post,* November 5, 2000.

Chapter 4

SECULAR SEARCH FOR PRINCIPLED GUIDANCE: This was the consensus of lay and clergy opinion at the Forum's final meeting, January 29, 2001.

CHURCH CRITIQUES OF NUCLEAR ARMS CONTROL: See, *e.g.,* Commission on Peace of the Episcopal Diocese of Washington, *The Nuclear Dilemma* (1985).

JUST-WAR PRINCIPLES: See Episcopal Inquiry Into Economic Sanctions, "Exploratory Essay," September 1997.

CONFERENCES ON RELIGION AND GLOBAL CONDUCT: William Pfaff, *Commonweal,* November 19, 1999.

INVASION OF GRENADA: Presentation of Robert Gallucci, dean of the Georgetown School of Foreign Service, at a University of Chicago Divinity School conference on "The Sacred and the Sovereign," October 20, 2000.

BOOTLESS PRONOUNCEMENTS: Episcopal Inquiry, *supra,* Part E.

"HYPOCRISY IS THE HOMAGE": Francois, duc de La Rochefoucauld, *Reflections* (1678), maxim 24.

Chapter 5

CHURCH DIPLOMACY: Forum presentation by Fr. John Langan, S.J., "The Place of Values in Foreign Affairs," April 22, 1998.

RELIGIOUS SUMMIT: Gustav Niebuhr, "World's Religious Figures Sign a Pledge for Peace," *New York Times*, September 1, 2000.

DEBT RELIEF: Forum debate, "Third World Debt Relief," October 23, 1998. See also Carrie Reiling, "Jubilee 2000: Churches on the Front Line," *Foreign Service Journal,* January 2001, pages 39-44.

HOLY LAND MEDIATION: Forum presentation by Major Charles A. Pfaff, U.S. Army. "Religion as a Source of Reconciliation in the Middle East," May 23, 2000.

INTERNATIONAL CENTER FOR RELIGION AND DIPLOMACY: See its brochure, available from 1156-15th Street, N.W., Suite 910, Washington, DC 20005.

NON-GOVERNMENTAL ORGANIZATIONS: Forum presentation by David Cohen, "The Role of NGO's in International Relations," April 11, 2000.

Chapter 6

AMERICA'S ROLE: Forum presentation by Roland Homet, "The Forgotten Virtues of Diplomatic Detachment," March 24, 1998.

SOUTH CAROLINA PRIMARY: Debate carried by CNN, February 2000.

EXCEPTIONALISM: Closing Forum discussion, January 29, 2001.

Chapter 7

WALTER McDOUGALL: "Introduction," in *Orbis* (Faith and Statecraft issue), Spring 1998, pages 162-63.

FR. BRYAN HEHIR: Presentation at a University of Chicago conference on "The Sacred and the Sovereign," October 20, 2000.

NATO EXPANSION: Forum presentation by Ambassador Jonathan Dean, "NATO Expansion: An Imbalance of Power?", June 25, 1998.

MISSILE DEFENSE: The view advanced by its proponents, that the regime of mutually assured deterrence no longer holds sway, has been refuted by the Republican and Democratic secretaries of defense responsible for ushering in the ABM Treaty. Robert McNamara and Thomas Graham, "Nuclear Arms Still Keep the Peace," The *New York Times,* July 15 2001; Melvin Laird, "Why Scrap the ABM Treaty?", *Washington Post,* August 23, 2001.

FOREIGN VIEWS OF MISSILE DEFENSE: *New York Times,* "Transition in Washington," January 20, 2001; James Dao, "Please Do Not Disturb Us With Bombs," *New York Times,* February 11, 2001; Trever Corson, "Backing Beijing Into a Corner," *New York Times,* March 12, 2001.

MISSILE DEFENSE AS A BARGAINING COUNTER: Forum presentation by Douglas Paal, "Encountering the New China," November 15, 2000.

SUITCASE ALTERNATIVE: *New York Times, op. cit.,* February 11, 2001.

JOSEF JOFFE: *New York Times,* June 20, 2000.

ALIENATING EFFECTS OF TRIUMPHALISM: Said & Funk, *Islam and the West, op. cit. supra.*

U.S. NEED FOR FOREIGN PARTNERS: Study by the RAND Corporation, 1997.

Chapter 8

RUSSIA: Forum presentation by Roland Homet, "Premature Efforts To Westernize Mother Russia," September 23, 1998.

PUTIN AND GORBACHEV: Patrick Tyler, "Russians Wonder if Putin Accepts Limits to Power," *New York Times,* August 14. 2000.

"ORDERED LIBERTY": See Roland Homet, *The New Realism* (1990), chapter 8.

POLITICAL CULTURE: *Ibid.*

CHINA: Forum presentation by Douglas Paal, "Encountering the New China," November 15, 2000.

SPY PLANE INCIDENT: The assertion of legal rights, much touted by both sides, was unlikely to settle the dispute. In 1968, France's NATO partners formally decided that France had the legal right to evict their forces and headquarters, but that doing so unilaterally was an "abuse of right" for which compensation was payable and was indeed paid.

Chapter 9

CONTROLS ON IRAQ: See the extensive coverage of this subject in the *New York Times* and the *Washington Post,* February-March 2001.

"ROGUE" TERMINOLOGY: Robert Litvak, "Rogue State: A Handy Label, but a Lousy Policy," *Washington Post,* February 20, 2000.

IRAN: Forum presentation by Ambassador Bruce Laingen, "Restoring Relations with Iran," June 29, 1999.

CONCILIATORY GESTURES: President Khatami's speech to the UN in 1999 called for a "dialogue of civilizations" between Iran and the West. *New York Times,* May 17, 1999.

IRANIAN ARMS DEAL WITH RUSSIA: *New York Times,* March 13, 2001.

NORTH KOREA: Forum presentation by Bradley Babson, "The Delicate Diplomacy with North Korea," November 30, 1999 (with associated topical outline).

"SUNSHINE POLICY": This aims for the demilitarization and eventual reunification of North and South Korea.

ISOLATING DICTATORS: David Sanger, "It's North Korea. Go Figure," *New York Times,* March 11, 2001.

TERRORISM: Stories and commentaries in the *New York Times* for January 16, February 10, and February 28, 2001. The September 11, 2001 attack on the World Trade towers and the Pentagon occupies a different class; among other things, its perpetrators procured their own publicity and martyrdom.

DRUG WARS: Forum presentation by Michael Massing, "Misadventures of the Drug War," June 14, 2000; *New York Times,* "Transition in Washington: International Choices," January 20, 2001.

Chapter 10

INTERVENTION IN DOMESTIC AFFAIRS: Forum summary of discussion, "The Forgotten Values of Diplomatic Detachment," March 24, 1998.

MILITARY INTERVENTION: Forum presentation by General Howard Graves, U.S. Army, "A Soldier's Perspective on U.S. Ideals and Interests Abroad," March 31, 1999; presentation of General James McCarthy, U.S. Air Force, conference on "The Sacred and the Sovereign," University of Chicago Divinity School, October 20, 2000.

MIDDLE-COUNTRY FORCES: General Lewis MacKenzie, Canadian Army, "A Crucial Job, But Not One for a Superpower," *Washington Post,* January 14, 2001.

POWELL AUTOBIOGRAPHY: *An American Journey* (1996), cited and quoted by Steven Mufson, *Washington Post,* December 16, 2000.

ECONOMIC SANCTIONS: Episcopal Inquiry Into Economic Sanctions, "Exploratory Essay," September 1997.

BOYCOTT OF IRAQ: Howard Schneider, "Ten Years On, Iraqis Shrug Off Embargo," *Washington Post,* February 24, 2001.

BUSH PRESS CONFERENCE: *Washington Post,* February 23, 2001.

REFUGEE FLOWS: Forum presentation by Kathleen Newland, "Post-Cold War Refugee and Asylum Policy," February 29, 2000. The *Washington Post* began a series on this topic on March 18, 2001.

OVERALL RECORD: Forum presentation by Roland Homet, "Assessing Humanitarian Intervention," September 30, 1999.

SOMALI STARVATION: *New York Times,* January 9, 2001.

PRESIDENT KOSTUNICA: *New York Times,* October 11, 2000.

INTERNATIONAL LAW: The informal poll was conducted by Forum member, and international lawyer, Arthur Downey.

Chapter 11

THEORY AND PRACTICE: The choices were described and developed at the Chicago Divinity School's conference on "The Sacred and the Sovereign," October 20, 2000.

SACRED vs. SOVEREIGN: "Sightings" service, Internet, September 2000.

PETER AND CORNELIUS: Acts 10.

NIEHBUR-MORGENTHAU DIALOGUE: John C. Bennett & Harvey Seifert, *U.S. Foreign Policy and Christian Ethics* (1977).

CHILD LABOR ABROAD: Forum presentation by Dr. Robert Dunn, "WTO Regulation of Labor and the Environment," October 28, 1999.

LEE YUAN KEW: *Newsweek* Special Issue, "The New Asia," Summer 2000.

CHINESE HUMAN RIGHTS REPORT: *New York Times,* February 28, 2001.

ROBERT D. KAPLAN: "Was Democracy Just a Moment," *The Coming Anarchy (2000).*

MACAULEY SPEECH: Episcopal Inquiry Into Economic Sanctions, "Exploratory Essay," September 1997.

KENNAN STATEMENT: *New York Review of Books,* Spring 1999.

Chapter 12

CRIMINAL PROSECUTION: Forum presentation by Hon. Monroe Leigh, "The Proposed International Criminal Court," January 27, 2000. After the events of September 11, 2001, a number of voices called for prosecuting the perpetrators in the International Criminal Court. They failed to notice: (a) that the Court was not yet in existence; (b) that it would have no jurisdiction over crimes committed before it came into existence; and (c) that the Court's framers could not agree on the definition of terrorism and so left the crime out of its mandate.

MINOR FIGURES: The notorious exception has been the last-minute extradition to The Hague, by Yugoslavia, of its former president Slobodan Milosevic—against the expressed judgment of its parliament, its Supreme Constitutional Court, and its newly elected president Vojislaka Kostunica, himself a constitutional lawyer. The action, which threatened the breakup of the reform government, was undertaken to secure a large but conditional offer of subsidy from the West, in effect a bribe. It was not a bright day for the rule of law. See, *e.g.*, Ian Fisher, "Where Justice Takes a Back Seat to Just Ending War," the *New York Times,* July 15, 2001.

ADAM MICHNIC: *New York Times Sunday Magazine,* November 9, 1999 (emphasis added).

RESTORATIVE JUSTICE: Forum presentation by Dr. David Little, "Restorative or Retributive Justice for Offenses Against Humanity," May 28, 1998. See also the May-June (1998) issue of *Church and Society,* devoted to "Forgiveness in Public Life."

THE MOVEMENT TO DOMESTIC HUMAN-RIGHTS PROCEEDINGS: See, *e.g.,* Carlotta Gall, "Milosevic Facing Arrest by Serbs for a Local Trial," *New York Times,* February 9, 2001; Tamar Lewin, "New Center To Aid Lands As They Heal Old Wounds," the *New York Times,* July 29, 2001

"DISGRACE TO CIVILIZATION": *New York Times* television review, May 1998.

Chapter 13

MODERNIZATION vs. TRADITIONAL CULTURE: Forum presentations by Dr. Larry Darby, "Globalization and Its Discontents," January 28, 1999, and by The Rev. Canon Michael Hamilton, "International Economic Challenges," October 26, 2000.

THOMAS FRIEDMAN: *From Beirut to Jerusalem* (1995 ed.), pages 549-50.

POLITICS OF GLOBALIZATION: Fareed Zakaria, "Globalization Grows Up and Gets Political," *New York Times,* December 31, 2000.

CHANGING DEMOGRAPHICS: Forum presentation by Dr. Colin Bradford, "Future Focus of Foreign Assistance," May 20, 1999.

EXPORTING DEMOCRACY: Forum presentation by Thomas Carothers, "Promoting Democracy Abroad," September 27, 2000.

DEMOCRACY CONFERENCE: Jane Perlez, coverage in the *New York Times,* January 26, 2000.

SCHOLAR-DIPLOMATS: Robert D. Kaplan, *The Coming Anarchy* (2000); Richard Haass, *The Reluctant Sheriff* (1997); Kishore Mahbumani, "The West and the Rest," *The National Interest,* Summer 1992; William Brandt, internal critique of Carothers' *Aiding Democracy Abroad* (Carnegie Endowment).

Chapter 14

PROFESSOR LAURENCE HARRISON: Presentation at the Inter-American Development Bank, November 10, 2000. See also Roland Homet, *The New Realism* (1990), page 8.

ISLAMIC REVIVAL: Abdul Aziz Said & Nathan C. Funk, *Islam and the West* (1998).

"GUN TO THE HEAD": Robert D. Kaplan, "Was Democracy Just a Moment," *op. cit. supra.*

RELIGIOUS FREEDOM ACT: David Jones, "The Joy of Sects: Religious Freedom Reporting," *Foreign Service Journal,* January 2001, pages 24-30.

About the Author

Roland Stevens Homet, Jr. is a lawyer and author who has been engaged in foreign diplomacy, religious inquiry, and study processes appropriate to each. He graduated *magna cum laude* from Harvard College and Harvard Law School, served as a Naval officer in Pacific and Atlantic waters, and then as a law clerk to Supreme Court Justice Felix Frankfurter. Mr. Homet practiced law with the Wall Street firm of Cleary, Gottlieb, Steen & Hamilton before turning to public service.

He has been engaged abroad in matters that involved NATO integrity, arms control, and the reconciliation of competing cultures. He organized and directed a foundation-sponsored project called "American Specialists on the Soviet Union," drawing scholars together on a systematic basis with U.S. policy makers and the press. His resulting book, *The New Realism* (1990), proposed a path to post-Cold War diplomacy.

Mr. Homet is an active Episcopalian, a member for several years of the executive committee of Forward Movement Publications, and author of its pamphlet on "The Role of the Church in Public Policy." He currently serves on the Peace Commission of the Diocese of Washington.

On occasion, Mr. Homet has made headway by bringing together people of differing views but reconcilable interests. He chaired committees of NATO and of UNESCO that managed to distill a productive harmony out of what had been a stalemated impasse. In other instances he has served as a public-interest moderator, for the Aspen Institute and in his own public television series, "Foreign Policy Choices 1996."